Diver and basking shark

100 Best Dives in Cornwall

by Charles Hood

A guide on the best places to dive from Looe to Padstow

This book is dedicated to Sandra my wife, best friend and long-time diving partner. Also to my children William and Samantha who will hopefully be the next generation of divers to explore the majestic waters found off the Cornish coastline.

Charles Hood

First published in the UK in 2003 by Circle Books
Circle Books
83/84 George Street
Richmond
Surrey TW9 1HE
Phone: 020 8332 2709

Design
Ian Legge

Print
Printed in China by Midas Printing International Ltd for Compass Press Limited
100-104 Upper Richmond Road
London SW15 2SP

ISBN: 0-9538919-3-3

Newquay

Pendeen lighthouse

Contents

Dive 10 Portnadler and Monkey Rock   Dive 14 Kanteong Dredger

The Dives

Dive 39 The John R Park

Dive 19 Lath Rock

Dive 91 Madusa Rock

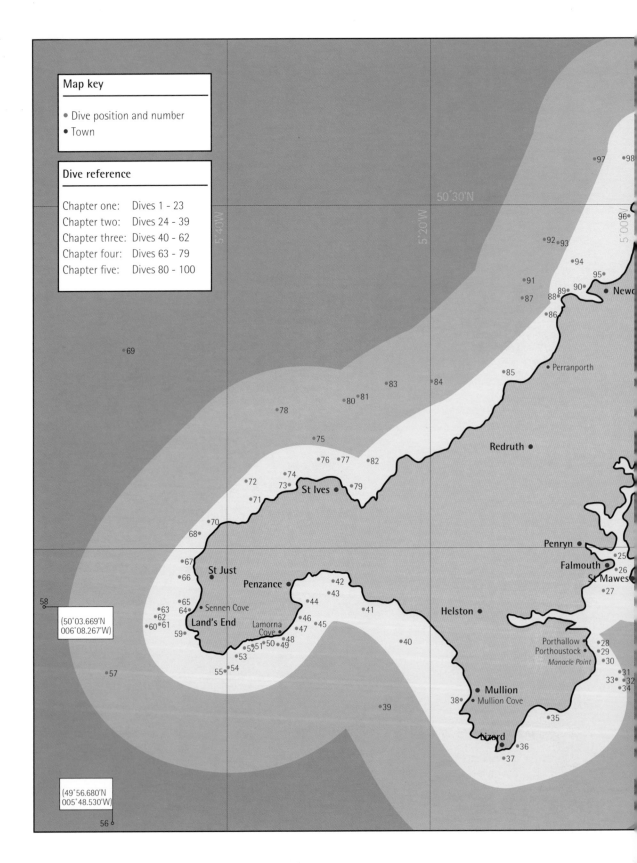

Map key

• Dive position and number
• Town

Dive reference

Chapter one:	Dives 1 - 23
Chapter two:	Dives 24 - 39
Chapter three:	Dives 40 - 62
Chapter four:	Dives 63 - 79
Chapter five:	Dives 80 - 100

50°30'N

5°40'W

5°20'W

5°00'W

•97   •98

96•

•92 •93

•94

95•

•91   89• 90•   •Newo
87•   88•

•86

•69

•85   • Perranporth

•83   •84

•80 •81

•78

Redruth •

•75

•76 •77   •82

•74
72• 73•   •79
•71   St Ives •

•70
68•

•67
66•   St Just •   Penryn •

Penzance •   •42   Falmouth •   •25
•43   •26
58   St Mawes
•   65• 44•   •27
(50°03.669'N   63• 64• • Sennen Cove
006°08.267'W) 62•   •41   Helston •
60• 61•   •46 •45
59• Land's End 47•   Porthallow •   •28
Lamorna •48   Porthoustock • •29
Cove 52• 50• •49   Manacle Point   •30
55•51   •31
•53   33• •32
55• 54•   •34
•57
•40
•35
• Mullion
38• • Mullion Cove
•39
Lizard •
•36
•37
(49°56.680'N
005°48.530'W)

56 ○

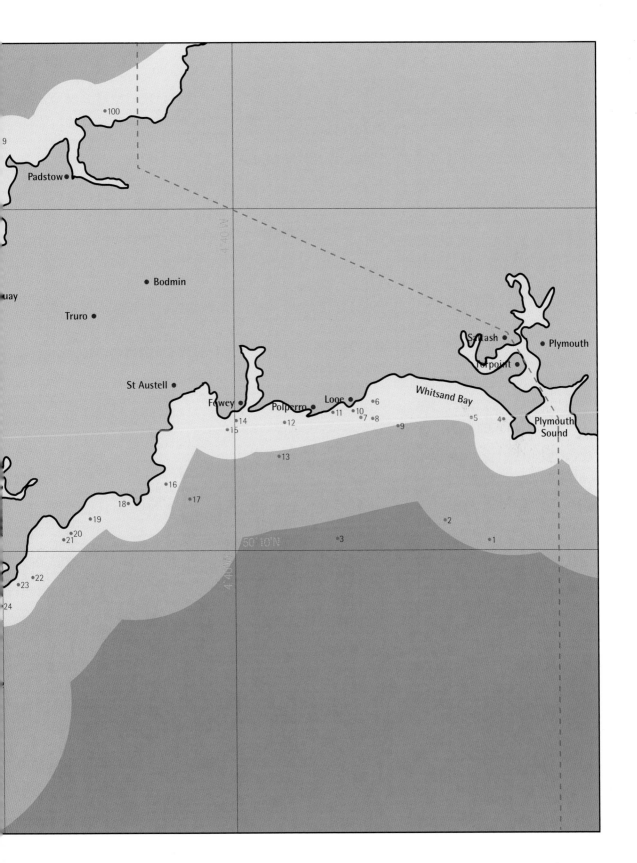

9

100

Padstow ●

● Bodmin

uay

Truro ●

Saltash ● Plymouth ●
Torpoint ●

St Austell ●

Fowey ●
Polperro ● Looe ● ● 6
● 14   ● 11 ● 10
● 12   ● 7 ● 8
● 15

Whitsand Bay
● 9

Plymouth
Sound

● 5   ● 4

● 13

● 16

18 ●   ● 17

19 ●

20 ●
21 ●

22 ●
23 ●

24

● 2

50°10'N   ● 3   ● 1

Introduction

What do you envisage when you think of Cornwall? Pirates, wreckers, smugglers, shipwrecks, violent storms and witchcraft usually spring to mind. Endless, lazy school summer holidays exploring golden, deserted beaches. Postcards, pasties and B&Bs. Landladies in farmhouses cooking up huge English breakfasts. Afternoon tea with scones, jam and clotted cream. All are quintessentially Cornwall. But there is one further majestic quality – the diving.

Over the past twenty years of diving Cornwall's coastline I have seen a huge diversity of marine life including dolphins, turtles, seals, blue sharks, sunfish, basking sharks and huge walls exquisitely covered in jewel anemones. One year I discovered where the cuttlefish breed in the summer months. I have witnessed superb visibility more associated with the Red Sea. I have had to be rescued by a passing fishing vessel after being swept from the dive site by a ferocious current. I have been capsized due to the sudden changeability of her weather. But I return every year. Why? Quite simply Cornwall has some of the best diving along England's coastline.

This guide then, is the best of the best - the top 100 dive sites. They range from easily accessible shallow shore dives where flat-fish proliferate to deep, intact wrecks right on the edge of sport diving capabilities. Number one on the list is the Eddystone reef situated 12 miles out to sea from Looe. Here the underwater terrain is dramatic, giving rise to fabulous anemone gardens. Huge shoals of mackerel, pollack and bass are also common. We then follow the coast past the famous wreck of the James Eagan Layne towards the Manacles and the Lizard Peninsula. Here are some of the most well-known

and popular sites in the whole of Cornwall: the wrecks of the Volnay and Mohegan and the spectacular pinnacles of Vase and Pen-win. Further west the coastline gets more dramatic. The sunlight takes on a mysterious quality, illuminating the hard, granite cliffs. Remote coves and smugglers' caves dot the shore and the diving is stunning.

The lighthouse at Land's End is subject to some of the most turbulent waters in the UK. The full force of the English Channel and Bristol Channel meet here twice a day. The result is a profusion of underwater life. Conger eels share their lairs with ling, lobsters roam the sea bed in search of better holes and sunfish float near the surface after riding in on the warm Gulf Stream. Dolphins visit frequently, feeding on shoals of mackerel. Heading north the guide takes us through the many wrecks found close to the shore. Many were torpedo victims from both the great wars, while others succumbed to fierce storms or thick fog. Due to the absence of large rivers on the north coast and the hard nature of the sea bed, the visibility is nearly always good.

The spectacular marine life found in Cornwall is there for one reason - the superb quality of the seawater. The warm Gulf Stream brings nutrient-rich waters from the south. These combine with the cooler waters from the English and Bristol Channels to form a cocktail of marine food that sustains a phenomenal chain of life. From the smallest phytoplankton the size of a pinhead to one of the largest animals at more than 6m in length - the basking shark - Cornwall supports a huge diversity of aquatic species.

How to use the guide

This is a guide for divers. It contains all the information required to select the type of diving you wish to do. The dive sites are split into five chapters according to their location. These begin at the at the south-east and follow the coastline anticlockwise around Land's End, ending in the north-east. Dives sites are headed-up by their category. This can be either wreck, reef, shore, drift or night dive or a combination of these. A minimum suggested level of competence follows. 'Novice' means anyone not qualified to dive without an instructor. 'Sport diver' means any diver qualified to dive with a diver of the same level or higher. 'Advanced' means a diver who has completed at least 50 open water dives, including a variety of differing conditions, and to a minimum depth of 30m. It then provides the maximum likely depth or range of depths the diver will experience. Following this is a suggestion of suitable slipways for a RIB on a trailer and then a list of diving shops or places to fill cylinders. It provides accurate GPS (Global Positioning System) positions to three decimal places – that is within about 5m. These are given as degrees, minutes and thousandths of minutes. A brief description includes the history of the wreck or topography of the dive. Additionally, any useful facilities such as car parking, cafés and toilets are listed. The 'How and When' sections give advice on currents, slack and a suggested route plus any specific advice needed to aid location of the site, such as marks or prominent features. Finally, the guide includes what you are likely to see, as well as any special features or marine life common to the dive to look out for.

As with all adventurous sports great care should be taken while diving. The guide has been designed to aid and assist the diver in choosing Cornwall's best diving locations. It is as complete as we could make it but it is not a replacement for good dive planning and safe diving practices. The exposure and strong currents around Cornwall's coastline are why the marine life is so profuse – it is these very conditions which can fool the unaware diver or coxswain. New visitors to the area are strongly advised to seek additional advice from local skippers, dive shops and the coastguard.

Short-spined sea scorpion

Eighty

Fanny Lambert

Type Wreck **Level** Advanced diver
Depth 44m

Launch Hayle
Air and dive shop Trevair, Undersea Adventures, Dive St Ives and Mount's Bay Diving

Position 50°19.560'N
005°28.590'W

Description
She was a 201ft-long, 699-ton, three-masted, steam cargo vessel which sank during a horrific storm on 6 February 1867 with total loss of life.

How/when to dive
The wreck must be dived on slack which is 30 minutes after high and low water Newquay.

What you are likely to see
It is fairly broken-up with two curiously square boilers. Underneath these lie the clearly visible remains of the brass helm which is jammed against the sea bed. Bib, pollack and whiting are common shoaling around what remains of its superstructure. She is also home to a suprising number of short-spined scorpion-fish.

Logan's Rock

Rockpool at Sennen

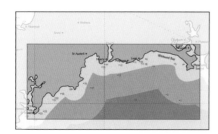

1 The Eddystone Lighthouse to St Anthony Head

The area between the Tamar and Fal rivers includes one of Cornwall's most famous dives – the wreck of the James Eagan Layne. Countless divers have enjoyed this stunning wreck which stands upright and remarkably intact in relatively sheltered and shallow water. It is also the site of the proposed deliberate sinking of a decommissioned naval vessel to create a replacement when the Layne finally breaks up. The offshore reefs of the Eddystone, Hand Deeps, Hatt Rock and Gull Rock also provide excellent dives. The coast is a mixture of sandy beaches and fishing villages – great for the visiting diver bringing the family. While one parent is diving, the other can entertain the children on the beach or stroll through the many seaside villages with their narrow and often cobbled streets. Here the pace of life is slow. The local residents are welcoming and provide high quality accommodation and food. These range from camp and caravan sites to five star hotels, as well as farmhouse bed and breakfasts. Almost every pub now stocks real ale and locally caught fresh fish is on most menus. As with many parts of Cornwall, bank holidays get busy. My advice is go when you can enjoy the tranquility and peacefulness. Divers are welcomed but please respect this hospitality. When driving a car with trailer and RIB through the narrow streets be considerate to other road users. Think carefully about the position and operation of any compressor. Respect the livelihoods of fishermen.

Lobster pot at low tide

1
One
Eddystone Reef

Type Reef **Level** Sport diver
Depth 0-40m

Launch Fort Bovisand, Mount Batten
Slip, Queen Anne's Battery,
Looe Harbour.
Air and dive shop Looe Divers

Position 50°10.750'N,
004°15.950'W

Description

The Eddystone reef is very easy to find as it is marked by a large lighthouse about 12 miles south of Plymouth Sound. There are a series of reefs running from east to west and the best diving is on the seaward side. In places these reefs break the surface and descend steeply to around 24m. At this depth sandy patches are broken-up by a further rocky reef that drops off to about 40m. There is plenty to explore over a number of dives.

How/when to dive

Diving can generally be carried out at all states of the tide as a lee can be found at the opposite side to the direction of the current. If diving on spring tides, it is advisable to dive on slack water – two and a half hours after high or low water Devonport.

What you are likely to see

There is a prolific amount of anemones, rose coral, dogfish and many species of wrasse, particularly mating cuckoo wrasse in late spring. Some years there is a profusion of brightly coloured, edible urchins. The first 10m is generally covered in a thick carpet of kelp during the summer months.

Male cuckoo wrasse

Spider crab

Two

Hand Deeps

Type Reef, drift dive option
Level Advanced diver **Depth** 12-50m

Launch Fort Bovisand,
Mount Batten Slip, Looe Harbour
and Queen Anne's Battery.
Air and dive shop Looe Divers

Position 50°12.580'N,
004°20.400'W

Description

Lying about three and half miles west-north-west of the Eddystone lighthouse is Hand Deeps. Legend has it that it was named by local fishermen observing the sea bed through the clear water who declared it to be a hand deep. In fact the shallowest part is around 8-10m. The reef is sprawled over 25,000sqm and consists of many gullies which start at 15m and descend to 40m. Towards the west these gullies are shallower and bottom out at 20 to 25m. The most prolific life can be found to the north on the shallowest part of Hand Deeps. It is marked to the west by a cardinal buoy.

How/when to dive

On good neaps Hand Deeps can be dived at all states of the tide. Experienced divers may wish to drift dive the site off slack. At springs it is strongly advisable to dive at slack water – two and a half hours after high and low water Devonport.

What you are likely to see

The area is similar to the Eddystone in marine life but the underwater topography is much more dramatic.

Three

Hatt Rock

Type Reef **Level** Advanced diver
Depth 24-50m

Launch Fort Bovisand, Looe Harbour,
Mount Batten Slip and
Queen Anne's Battery.
Air and dive shop Looe Divers

Position 50°10.600'N
004°29.300'W

Description

This is a flat-topped pinnacle at 24m, so named as it resembles the appearance of a top hat. The sides of the pinnacle, which are sheer in many places, descend to 70m. This is one of the most spectacular scenic dives in this part of Cornwall. Due to its depth it makes a good deep-dive training site with plenty of marine life to observe.

How/when to dive

On good neaps it can be dived at all states of the tide. At springs it can only be dived at slack water which is two and a half hours after high and low water Devonport.

What you are likely to see

The marine life here is also similar to that found on the Eddystone, although due to its depth there is little kelp. One noticeable difference is that there are usually large shoals of mackerel and pollack to be found each end of slack water. This is an awe-inspiring site with some dramatic drop-offs and excellent walls. The visibility is usually in excess of 10m and in springs at late summer can be over 25m.

Diver photographing Hatt Rock

Plumose anemones

Forward hold   Descending into the engine-room

Best wreck dive

4

Four

SS James Eagan Layne

Type Wreck **Level** Sport diver
Depth 7-24m

Launch Fort Bovisand, Looe Harbour,
Mount Batten Slip and
Queen Anne's Battery.
Air and dive shop Looe Divers.

Position 50°19.533-601'N
004°14.723'W

Description

At 442ft and 10,414 tons deadweight she was a World War Two American Liberty ship. Built by women labourers, these merchant ships were designed for a one-way trip to England carrying much needed supplies. Unfortunately the James Eagan Layne was torpedoed by U-624 (Oberleutnant Cordes) between No.4 hold and No.5 hold on the starboard side on 21 March 1945. An attempt was made to beach her but she sank about a mile from shore in Whitsand Bay, just west of Plymouth. The wreck now lies upright with the bow in 20m of water and the stern in 24m.

How/when to dive

The 'James', as the wreck is locally referred to, may be dived at virtually any time of day. The only current I have experienced is around its bow on a spring tide, however it is quite easy to swim against. About 70m to the stern lies a large red cardinal wreck-buoy making it quite easy to find with a good echo-sounder.

What you are likely to see?

The James is starting to open up now. When I first dived the wreck its mast was still sticking out of the water and many of its holds could not be entered. However, this does not mean this is not still a great dive. For me it is still one of the finest on the south coast

Wagon wheels

Bow

of Cornwall. The relatively shallow depth and huge size make this a superb first and second dive and ideal for an advanced training site. The bow rises to about 6m and is covered in white plumose anemones and dead man's fingers. There are plenty of opportunities to carry out easy penetration dives as the wreck is relatively intact until aft of its engine-room. Take care not to dislodge any loose girders or plates as these are rusting badly in places. The engine-room has collapsed but surrounding it there is still plenty of evidence of the cargo, especially large gun-carriage wheels. The stern lies about 20m south-west of the main wreck and is usually covered in fish life.

Transit points

If you are approaching the James Eagan Layne by RIB or hard boat and have no GPS to guide you, here are some useful transit marks to help locate the wreck

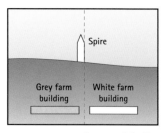

Prominent building on horizon

White hut half-way up cliff

Common transit looking approximately 015 degrees (M)

Radio mast

Cleft at base of cliff

Bow section looking 110 degrees (M)

Spire

Grey farm building

White farm building

Stern transit looking 105 degrees (M)

Five

SS Rosehill

Type Wreck **Level** Sport diver
Depth 30m

Launch Fort Bovisand, Looe Harbour,
Mount Batten Slip and
Queen Anne's Battery.
Air and dive shop Looe Divers

Position 50°19.660'N
004°18.416- 433'W

Description

This British-owned armed merchant ship, 314ft-long and weighing 2,788 tons, was torpedoed by the German submarine UB-40 on 23 September 1917. She eventually sank in Whitsand Bay with her 3,980-ton cargo of coal. The wreck lies in about 30m of water among a series of rocky outcrops making it difficult to find. It is now quite broken-up but its boilers are still intact.

How/when to dive

As it is difficult to find, a set of marks are given below. Line the first mark up and use the second to pinpoint the wreck. The problem with the second mark is that it varies with the state of the tide as shown. In practice it may take several runs but the boilers do show up pretty well on the echo-sounder when right over them.

What you are likely to see

The wreck is lying virtually upside down and generally the visibility is poor at an average of 5m. The engine-room has opened up and around the two boilers is a huge jumble of metal. At the bow is an anchor and chain and part of a mast complete with the pulleys. There are usually quite a few lobster, large conger and shoals of bib to be found all through the summer months.

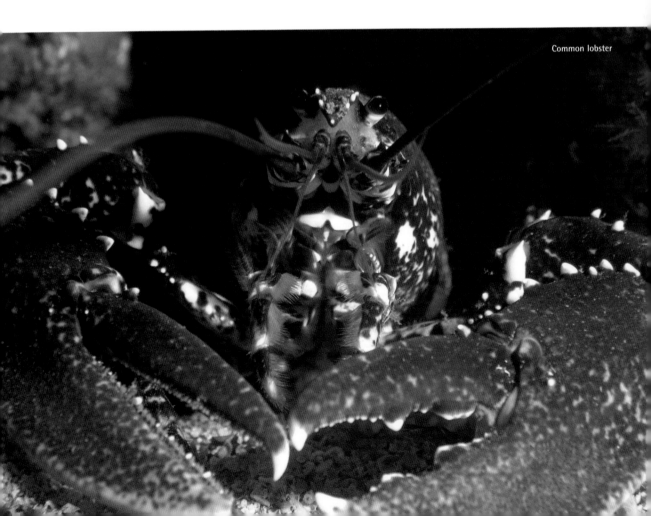

Common lobster

Corkwing wrasse

Location of SS Rosehill

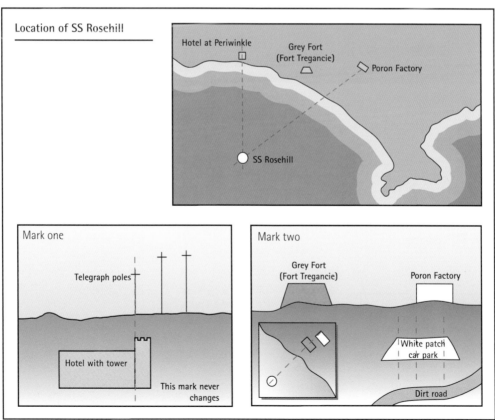

Hotel at Periwinkle

Grey Fort
(Fort Tregancie)

Poron Factory

SS Rosehill

Mark one

Telegraph poles

Hotel with tower

This mark never changes

Mark two

Grey Fort
(Fort Tregancie)

Poron Factory

White patch
car park

Dirt road

Scallop

Gosse anemone

Grey seal

Six

Marine Drive and Basket Rock

Type Shore and night
Level Novice diver **Depth** 9m

Air and dive shop Looe Divers

Position Marine Drive has several access points to the sea just in front of the Looe Divers shop.

Description

The Voluntary Marine Conservation Area covers the area 40m from shore and can easily be dived. Close to the coastguard station is the wreck of Naiad, a sailing schooner which floundered in 1931 and is now broken-up.

How/when to dive

Diving is possible at any state of the tide although around high water are the easiest entry and exit conditions. An SMB is required for this dive due to the local boat traffic. There is little or no current.

What you are likely to see

At the heart of the reef is Basket Rock which is surrounded by rocks and gullies giving easy opportunities to explore or photograph the beautiful marine life which includes ballan wrasse, pipefish, spider crabs, cuttlefish, lobster and bass. Occasionally you might get your fins nibbled by a one-eyed resident seal called Nelson.

Plaice

Seven

Looe Island and Zanussi Reef

Type Reef **Level** Novice diver
Depth 5-20m

Launch Looe Harbour
Air and dive shop Looe Divers

Position 50°20.250'N
004°26.800'W and
50°20.650'N
004°25.800'W

Description

Located about 600m from the shore at Marine Drive is Looe Island, the heart of Looe's Voluntary Marine Conservation Area. Less than three quarters of a mile to the east is an anchoring ground. Over the years many ships have thrown or lost various artefacts over the side. Today some interesting finds are occasionally made.

How/when to dive

Looe Island can be dived at any state of the tide and irrespective of where the wind is coming from as it always provides shelter. If conditions permit the best diving is on the south side.

What you are likely to see

There are many gullies and sheltered reefs harbouring the usual marine life that is found in the general area (see Marine Drive). The visibility is generally good even after recent bad weather. This makes quite a good site for training dives. Towards Zanussi Reef the sea bed deepens to around 20m and is relatively sandy. Flatfish and scallops are common while there is always a chance of finding some lost treasure!

Eight

The Ranneys

Type Reef **Level** Novice diver
Depth 12-20m

Launch Looe Harbour
Air and dive shop Looe Divers

Position 50°20.000'N
004°26.600'W

Description

The Ranneys are a series of rocks that run some 400m south-east of Looe Island. Many ships have floundered here over the years, including galleons dating back to the Spanish Armada.

How/when to dive

There can be a reasonably strong current flowing so it is best to dive at slack which is at high or low water Looe. Alternatively off slack it makes a great drift dive. Note there are many uncharted rocks in the area so coxswains should keep a sharp eye out, especially at low tide.

What you are likely to see

The strong current affords a profusion of marine life similar to Marine Drive but in greater density and variety. Many of the gullies are filled with bits of wreckage and there are some iron cannon-balls to be found. There is no point in trying to retrieve these as they will disintegrate as soon as they start to dry.

Sagartia anemone

Red fingers

Nine **9**

Crystal Reef

Type Reef and drift
Level Advanced diver **Depth** 15-40m

Launch Looe Harbour
Air and dive shop Looe Divers

Position see the 20m contour line
on a chart

Description

Crystal Reef is the local name given to a huge reef system which extends from Looe Island east for about five miles. It runs roughly parallel to the coastline about two miles off. The top of the reef is at about 15m which then rapidly descends to 30-40m. The best way is to explore the area with a good echo-sounder and choose your spot.

How/when to dive

There can be a reasonably strong current flowing so it is best to dive at slack which is at high or low water Looe. Alternatively, off slack it makes a great drift dive for experienced divers.

What you are likely to see

Usually very clear water surrounds a series of walls, ledges and pinnacles. Scallops are quite common in deeper water. In places there are huge amounts of Ross coral, gorgonian coral and red fingers. It is not uncommon to find lobster and large edible crab here as well. This area also makes an ideal deep water training site.

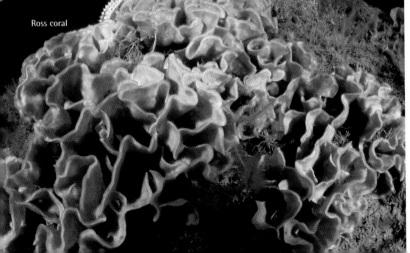

Ross coral

Dogfish

Ten 10

Portnadler and Monkey Rock or Hore Stone

Type Reef, shore or boat
Level Novice diver **Depth** 10m

Launch Looe Harbour
Air and dive shop Looe Divers

Position 50°20.080'N
004°28.420'W

Description
Monkey Rock lies just offshore and is the start of a pretty, shallow dive all the way to Portnadler. Portnadler is a sheltered cove situated between Looe and Talland Bay. It is a perfect site for training dives from the shore or by boat.

How/when to dive
Start off on the inside of Monkey Rock and follow the coastline eastwards which will bring you into Portnadler.

What you are likely to see
There are plenty of kelp-topped gullies to explore which are home to gobies, wrasse, spider crab, dogfish and a whole host of small anemones and corals. In the middle of the bay the sea bed turns to sand and is home to quite a few flatties. This is an ideal training area.

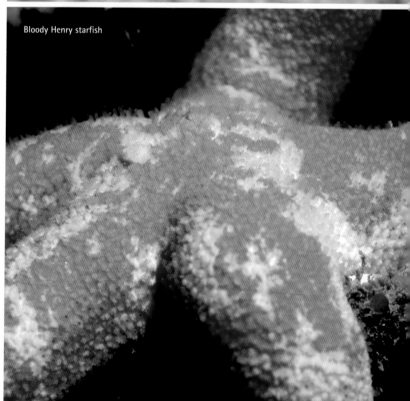
Bloody Henry starfish

11

Eleven

Talland Bay and trawler Marguerite

Type Reef, wreck, night and shore
Level Novice diver **Depth** 8m

Launch Looe Harbour
Air and dive shop Looe Divers

Position 50°20.105'N
004°29.760'W

Description
Two miles to the west of Looe is the idyllic cove of Talland Bay. Here there is ample parking, camping facilities and licensed cafés.

How/when to dive
The beach is largely covered at high water so you should plan a dive for a falling or low tide which will make entry easier. There are good reefs both to the east and west of the bay which support an interesting selection of aquatic life and a depth of 14-16m can be reached quite close to shore.

What you are likely to see
Usually the visibility is in excess of 10m and being so shallow makes an ideal training site. The remains of the 220-ton Marguerite, a French trawler which ran ashore on 3 May 1922 are scattered over the rocks. At low tide its boilers break the surface. The remains of two other wrecks can also be found among the gullies - those of the West Indiaman Tregothic and the Austrian brig Ester, which sank 10 January 1786 and March 1885 respectively. They are, however, very broken-up and only bits of twisted metal and the odd plate can be seen.

Close-up of the eye of a dogfish

12

Twelve

Udder Rock and SS White Rose

Type Reef, wreck and drift
Level Sport diver **Depth** 8-25m

Launch Looe Harbour, Bodinnick and Fowey.
Air and dive shop Looe Divers and Fowey Diving Services

Position 50°19.900'N
004°33.810'W

Description

Udder Rock is marked to seaward by a south cardinal buoy. To find the rock first position your boat slightly inshore of the buoy. Then look directly to shore and line up a patch of white rocks with a white marker. Head in on this bearing until the echo-sounder rises sharply. Note the rock dries on low water springs.

How/when to dive

The area can be dived at all states of the tide but on spring tides it becomes a drift dive.

What you are likely to see

The rock has a series of ledges running around it full of marine life – dogfish are particularly common in the spring. The rock makes an ideal multilevel dive and training site. To the seaward side is the anchor and chain of the SS White Rose which hit Udder Rock on 5 February 1901. Contrary to many reports the rest lies very well broken-up much further inshore near Nealand Point.

13

Thirteen

Folk Horn Rock or Owen Rock and SS Orchis

Type Reef and wreck
Level Advanced diver **Depth** 30-46m

Launch Looe Harbour, Bodinnick and Fowey.
Air and dive shop Looe Divers and Fowey Diving Services

Recorded position 50°16.730'N
004°34.330'W

Bib

Description

Owen Rock is a sheer-walled pinnacle similar to Hatt Rock but in slightly deeper water. It makes a good alternative to Hatt Rock if the weather conditions are rough. The wreck of the SS Orchis lies about 200m to the south-west of the rock at 50°16.778'N 004°34.619'W. She was a 482-ton steamship built in 1917 which sank 30 November 1936 after springing a leak off Gribbin Head. The wreck lies at 44m on a sand sea bed with its cargo of china clay. The highest point is around the midships at 40m.

How/when to dive

Best dived on slack water which is two and a half hours after high and low water Devonport.

What you are likely to see

The walls are covered in rich marine life and like the other off-shore sites visibility is generally very good. The wreck is upright on an even keel but in two parts. It is quite difficult to locate. The bow to midships is fairly intact but the stern is fairly well broken-up. There is a single boiler just forward of a mangled prop. There is usually a large shoal of bib swimming around its superstructure.

14

Fourteen

Kanteong Dredger

Type Wreck **Level** Novice diver
Depth 14m

Launch Looe Harbour, Bodinnick,
Fowey, Charlestown, Pentewan Sands,
Portmellon and Gorran Haven.
Air and dive shop Looe Divers,
Fowey Diving Services and Ocean Sports.

Position 50°18.832'N
05°39.084'W

Description

The 225ft by 75ft, 3,500-ton Kanteong
was the world's largest tin dredger
in her day. She was on tow from the
builder's yard in Holland bound for the
Far East when she capsized in a storm
off the Eddystone. She was abandoned
and drifted down the coast to Fowey
where she sank on 8 March 1937.
A salvage attempt of the bucket chain
and fittings was not very successful
and most remain on the sea bed in
position 50°18.917'N 004°39.167'W and
50°19.300'N 004°39.267'W.

How/when to dive

You can dive at any state of the tide.

What you are likely to see

The wreck settled on the sea bed in
two distinct parts. At low water, a huge
iron gear-wheel can be seen above the
surface close inshore. The shallow part
of the wreck can be found seaward of
this. There are usually large shoals of fish
hiding in the many nooks and crannies
provided by the broken-up wreckage.
This makes quite a good training site.

15

Fifteen

Cannis Rock

Type Reef **Level** Novice diver
Depth 6-10m

Launch Looe Harbour, Bodinnick,
Fowey, Charlestown, Pentewan Sands,
Portmellon and Gorran Haven.
Air and dive shop Looe Divers, Fowey
Diving Services and Ocean Sports.

Position 50°18.680'N
004°40.007'W

Description

Cannis Rock dries at low water spring tides, and is marked to seaward by a cardinal buoy. It is at the end of a reef system which extends right up to the shoreline.

How/when to dive

You can dive at all states of the tide, although there can be some current on spring tides. Make sure you fly the A flag in a prominent position as this site is a popular spot with anglers.

What you are likely to see

The reef system is full of gullies - many of which are filled with bright sand which reflects the sunlight greatly increasing the visibility. Fish life is usually very good with many species of wrasse, pollack, whiting and occasionally

Gosse anemone

Diving in clear water

Sixteen 16

Gwineas Reef

Type Reef **Level** Novice diver
Depth 15m

Launch Bodinnick, Fowey, Charlestown,
Pentewan Sands, Portmellon
and Gorran Haven.
Air and dive shop Fowey Diving
Services and Ocean Sports.

Position 50°14.685'N
004°45.695'W

Description
This well-known site just around the
bay from Mevagissey is worth visiting.
It is a good inshore site for the first
dive of the season and usually has a
profusion of fish and invertebrate life.
To the north-east, at the bottom of a
drop-off, lie the broken-up remains of
the SS Caroni River.

How/when to dive
This is diveable at all states of the tide.

What you are likely to see
It has plenty of fish life including many
different species of wrasse. There are
many gullies and swim-throughs
providing hiding places for crabs and
cuttlefish, while flounders and lemon
sole are often seen towards the sea bed.
There is a reef system that continues all
the way to Pen-a-maen which is ideal
for underwater photographers.

Flounder

Cuttlefish

17

Seventeen

SS Eastfield

Type Wreck **Level** Advanced diver
Depth 42-53m

Launch Looe Harbour, Bodinnick,
Fowey, Charlestown, Pentewan Sands,
Portmellon, Gorran Haven
and Portholland.
Air and dive shop Looe Divers, Fowey
Diving Services and Ocean Sports.

Position 50°14.255'N
004°42.262'W

Description
The SS Eastfield was an armed steamship
of of 2,150 gross tons. She was torpedoed
by the German submarine UB-57 during
the First World War on 27 November 1917
just off Dodman Point.

How/when to dive
The Eastfield can be dived on neaps at
almost all states of the tide. On springs it
is best dived up to one and a half hours
either side of slack which is about mid-
tide on ebb or flood.

What you are likely to see
The wreck basically lies upright with its
bow some 8m proud of the sea bed.
Other parts of it are also relatively intact
- especially the boilers and engine-room,
although the midships has collapsed.
It carried a cargo of coal which remains
strewn over the sea bed.

Dahlia anemone

Eighteen

Hemmick Beach

Type Reef and shore
Level Novice diver **Depth** 9m

Air and dive shop Ocean Sports.
Position 50°13.620'N
004°48.800'W

Description

This gently shelving reef from the shore and is ideal for training dives and photography.

How/when to dive

Follow the road out of Gorran Churchtown towards Boswinger, then keep right until you come to the beach. Drop off the gear and park in either of the two car parks close by. Access is easiest at high tide.

What you are likely to see

To the south-east of the bay the sand is replaced by a shallow reef system. Here the kelp is broken by gullies which shelter a whole host of juvenile marine life. In the summer months cuttlefish, flat-fish and whiting are common. In late spring ballan wrasse and corkwing wrasse breed in the shallow water.

Edible crab hiding in the sand

19

Nineteen

Lath Rock

Type Reef **Level** Sport diver
Depth 6-18m

Launch Portmellon, Gorran Haven,
Portholland, Pendower, St Mawes,
St Just, Mylor, Falmouth and
Mawnan Smith.
Air and dive shop Ocean Sports,
Seaways , Cornish Diving
and Haven Scuba.

Position 50°12.616'N
004°52.155'W

Description

This offshore, submerged rock consists
of a series of gullies and spectacular
walls. It is often described as difficult to
find. Using the GPS marks above and a
good echo-sounder there should be no
problems locating it.

How/when to dive

The rock can generally be dived at all
states of the tide, but on springs slack is
four hours before and two hours after
high water Devonport.

What you are likely to see

There is a great deal of marine life
around with many species of anemone,
coral and sponge. In late summer the fish
life can be quite prolific with shoaling
mullet not uncommon. The best visibility
tends to be on the flood tide and a little
current will bring out all the anemones.

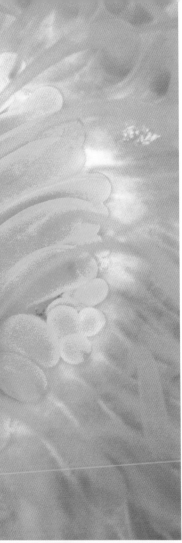

Twenty

The Hera and Gull Rock

Type Reef and wreck **Level** Sport diver
Depth 18m

Launch Portmellon, Gorran Haven,
Portholland, Pendower, St Mawes,
St Just, Mylor, Falmouth, Mawnan Smith
Air and dive shop Ocean Sports,
Seaways, Cornish Diving and Haven Scuba.

Position 50°11.880'N
004°54.017'W

Description

The Hera was a 280ft, 1,994-ton four-masted steel barque built in Tecklenburg in Germany, originally named the Richard Wagner. She struck the Whelps reef during a south-westerly gale on 1 February 1913. She managed to stay afloat and sail just a quarter of a mile before she sank on the west side of Gull Rock.

How/when to dive

This is diveable at any state of the tide.

What you are likely to see

The hull is in two virtually separate halves, with the remains of the masts to lead you from one to the other. In places the wreckage stands 5m up from the sea bed. There are plenty of plumose anemones and dead man's fingers which attract a wide variety of fish life. The central section of the hull is largely collapsed, although the ribs and decking are easily distinguished. In places the hull forms large iron caves big enough to swim into and where huge pollack hide. In good visibility light filters in from holes in the plating, lighting up shoals of small fish and making the whole experience quite surreal. The Hera is a surprisingly compact but picturesque wreck and it is often buoyed in the summer months.

Plumose anemone

Cuttlefish in kelp forest

21
Twenty-one

The Whelps

Type Reef **Level** Sport diver
Depth 10-27m

Launch Portmellon, Gorran Haven,
Portholland, Pendower, St Mawes,
St Just, Mylor, Falmouth and
Mawnan Smith.
Air and dive shop Ocean Sports,
Seaways, Cornish Diving
and Haven Scuba.

Position 50°10.390'N
004°54.515'W

Description

The Whelps is a series of peaks and gullies that just break the surface south of Gull Rock. The depth quickly drops to around 27m with many superb steep-sided walls.

How/when to dive

The Whelps can generally be dived at all states of the tide although on springs there is often a strong current on the seaward side.

What you are likely to see

The walls are full of sponges and soft corals while towards the bottom gorgonian fan coral and Ross coral are quite common. Fish are generally abundant with wrasse and shoals of pollack and whiting ever-present. Cuttlefish can often be seen hiding in sandy crevices during the summer. Visibility is usually excellent even after a storm as the sea bed consists of coarse sand and shingle.

Triggerfish

Tern

Triggerfish

Plumose anemone

22
Twenty-two

The Bizzies

Type Reef and drift **Level** Sport diver
Depth 10-17m

Launch Portholland, Pendower,
St Mawes, St Just, Mylor, Falmouth
and Mawnan Smith.
Air and dive shop Ocean Sports,
Seaways, Cornish Diving
and Haven Scuba.

Position 50°09.600'N
004°57.250'W

Description

The Bizzies is a similar dive to the
Old Wall (Dive 24) and not far away as
you see from the position. The reef is
lower and comprises a series of ledges
and gullies.

How/when to dive

This site is quite tidal but can be dived
at almost any time on a good neap. On
springs they should only be dived on
slack which is four hours before and two
hours after high water Devonport.

What you are likely to see

The area is similar in life and conditions
to the Old Wall - just a little shallower
and closer to shore. However, due to
the tide running stronger on springs
the anemones are in better condition
and more numerous here.

Slack water

Juvenile cuttlefish

23

Twenty-three

Killigerran Head

Type Reef and night **Level** Novice diver
Depth 8-12m

Launch Portholland, Pendower,
St Mawes, St Just, Mylor, Falmouth
and Mawnan Smith.
Air and dive shop Ocean Sports,
Seaways, Cornish Diving and
Haven Scuba.

Position 50°09.050'N
004°58.510'W

Description
This is a scenic, shallow site which makes it ideal for a second or training dive. In late summer visibility can be more than 10m making it a good spot for photography. The cliffs run straight into the water and below the surface you will encounter an extensive reef system of deep gullies and tunnels running out from the base of the cliffs.

How/when to dive
You can dive at all states of the tide.

What you are likely to see
The sea bed is fairly heavy shingle, so visibility is often very good even after a storm. Between the kelp there are plenty of juvenile fish and a host of different species of wrasse. There are often plenty of small critters on the walls and in the crevices of the gullies.

2

Falmouth Bay and
The Lizard Peninsula

Falmouth's fame as a shipping port is well documented. For many mariners it was the first major port on the south coast in which shelter could be found and repairs carried out after a long sea voyage. Thus it is hardly surprising that of all England's coastline, the Lizard Peninsula - with her dangerous Manacles reef - has one of the highest concentration of shipwrecks. At many times of the year when the rest of the country enjoys sunshine the Lizard is covered in mist or fog. The relatively warm, humid air from the Atlantic hits the high, cool cliffs and a thick sea mist forms. On reading the accounts of the many wrecks it is therefore not surprising to find fog as the main reason for loss. However, at the shoreline the sun usually breaks through the sea mist giving this part of Cornwall's coastline some of the longest sunshine hours and conditions can be perfect for diving. The prevailing wind is from the south-west and the east-facing Manacles are mainly sheltered by the land. The current can be strong but on a neap tide there is ample time to dive on slack water.

Author's daughter
Samantha snorkels with
a 6m basking shark

The author's wife Sandra and anglerfish

24 Twenty-four

The Old Wall

Type Reef **Level** Sport diver
Depth 20-35m

Launch Pendower, St Mawes, St Just, Mylor, Falmouth, Mawnan Smith, Porthkerris and Porthoustock.
Air and dive shop Seaways, Cornish Diving, Haven Scuba, Dive Action and Porthkerris Divers.

Position 50°74.400'N
004°59.900'W

Description

Approximately a mile offshore from Killigerran Head begins a reef system known locally as the Old Wall. The best diving in this area is found at the north-eastern edge of the reef where it runs a little deeper, but forms a series of semi-isolated pinnacles. The top of the reef here begins in 20-24m, which then drops off dramatically via a series of sheer faces and gullies to around 35m.

How/when to dive

The area is exposed to tidal movement and currents can be extremely strong, especially during spring tides, so choose to dive here at slack water or perhaps drift on a neap tide. Slack water is at one hour after or four hours before high water Devonport.

What you are likely to see

The rock faces are densely covered with dead man's fingers, gorgonian corals, jewel and plumose anemones and sponges. Where the rock meets the heavy, sand sea bed angler-fish are often encountered and large shoals of pollack and pouting are common.

Twenty-five

SS Stanwood

Type Wreck **Level** Sport diver
Depth 14-27m

Launch St Mawes, St Just, Falmouth,
Mylor, Mawnan Smith, Porthkerris
and Porthoustock.
Air and dive shop Seaways,
Cornish Diving, Haven Scuba,
Dive Action and Porthkerris Divers.

Position 50°10. 317' N
   005°02.101'W

Description

The Stanwood was a 4,158-ton, 240ft
steamship which sank on 10 December
1939 after her cargo of coal caught fire.
The wreck was quite heavily salvaged
so is now very broken-up. It lies on the
north bank in the Carrick Roads section
of Falmouth Harbour.

How/when to dive

The Stanwood is nearly always dived
when the weather is too rough to
venture outside the harbour. Because of
its location permission to dive it must be
sought from the harbour master.

What you are likely to see

The remains are scattered over a
gentle slope starting from around
14m. It is fairly well flattened but
lumps of coal can still be found, as
well as large sections of wreckage. At
27m – the deepest part - you can see
girders festooned with large plumose
anemones. Old lobsters and congers can
often be found hiding in the pipework,
but the silty conditions can result in
poor visibility.

Plumose anemones

26

Twenty-six

The Steps and U-boats

Type Reef, wreck and shore **Level** Novice diver **Depth** 10-12m

Air and dive shop Seaways , Cornish Diving, Haven Scuba.

Position Pendennis Point – Falmouth

Shore diving in the early days

Description

Deeply fissured reefs with sandy plains and U-boat wrecks are found within 50-100m of the shore. This is an ideal area for training, photography or keeping fit over the winter.

How/when to dive

Pendennis Point is a stone's throw from the centre of Falmouth town and has adequate parking and easy access to the water from the road. The best entry point is from the eastern end of Castle Beach where there is a small car park on the cliff top and steps leading down to the waters' edge. The U-boat wrecks are quite easy to find and there are the remains of five subs on the south-western side of the point within fifty yards of the shore. To find the closest wreck enter via the steps and follow the reef edge on your left approximately 50m out. Turn left and swim a further 50m or so parallel to the shore until you come to the first well-defined gully running out at right angles to the shore. Here you will find the remains of the pressure hull of the

first U-boat with other fair-sized pieces of wreckage close by. If you continue swimming east you will encounter the remains of two further submarines in the gullies between 50-100m from the shore, the farthest one perhaps 200m from your entry point. If you choose to dive directly from the rocks further up the road then make sure it is over the high water period as it is all too easy to get stranded by the falling tide and you may have a long swim to a suitable exit point.

What you are likely to see

Male corkwing wrasse are not the boldest of reef residents, but in spring some may allow a closer approach as they are engrossed in nest building all around Pendennis Point. You will normally spot them scavenging at the edge of the reef for bits of loose weed and other debris which they will pick up in their mouths and then transport to the nest site. However, one of the strangest fish you may encounter in spring is the male lumpsucker who is left in shallow

water guarding and nurturing his egg clutch after mating. These fish were apparently once common in the south-west, as they still are in the North Sea, but are now infrequently encountered. Metal remains of World War I German U-boats which were wrecked in 1920 are everywhere. One particular piece of wreckage, which was formerly part of the hydroplane assembly of a submarine, is a microcosm of reef life in itself. Aside from its temporary and permanently resident fish the underside is decorated with sponges, hydroids, tunicates, tube worms, cup corals and anemones and amongst these are often found topknot flatfish, clinging upside down like freestyle climbers. The top of the steelwork is covered with kelp, so from above it is indistinguishable from the reef itself. Among the fronds are swimming crabs, hermits, prawns and well camouflaged scorpionfish. Other camouflaged residents include the greater pipefish and snake pipefish - both of which hang around in the weed and you need sharp eyes to spot.

Dragonet

27

Twenty-seven

SS N.G. Peterson

Type Wreck and night
Level Sport diver **Depth** 21m

Launch St Mawes, St Just, Falmouth, Mylor, Mawnan Smith, Porthkerris and Porthoustock.
Air and dive shop Seaways, Cornish Diving, Haven Scuba, Dive Action and Porthkerris Divers.

Position 50°07.103'N
005°03.017'W

Description
This 1,282-ton, 239ft-long Danish steamship sank after colliding with the Norwegian SS Siri on 13 March 1918, along with her cargo of iron ore. Now it is very broken-up and resembles more of a scrapyard than a shipwreck.

How/when to dive
This is diveable at all states of the tide on neaps.

What you are likely to see
Although the site is hardly recognisable as a wreck and frequently offers poor visibility, bits of iron plates and pipes provide shelter for a huge variety of marine life. Curiously conger eels seem to have adopted this wreck as theirs – there are hundreds of them! Cuttlefish, bib, pollack and blennies are also quite common. Moreover, the Peterson really comes alive at night, so for local clubs it is a favourite site for night diving.

28 Twenty-eight

The Volnay

Type Wreck **Level** Sport diver
Depth 21m

Launch St Mawes, St Just, Mylor, Falmouth, Mawnan Smith, Porthkerris and Porthoustock.
Air and dive shop Seaways, Cornish Diving, Haven Scuba, Dive Action and Porthkerris Divers.

Position 50°04.331'N
005°03.857'W

Description

The Volnay was a 385ft, 4,610 gross tonnage armed cargo ship which sank on 14 December 1917 after hitting a mine under No.1 hold – probably laid by the German submarine UC-64. The wreck now sits upright although well broken-up. It features quite heavily in local history. People lived well from all the luxury goods washed ashore which included perfume, tinned meat and fruit, flour and other foodstuffs – all of which had been in short supply at the time.

How/when to dive

The Volnay is diveable at all states of the tide and her two larger boilers show quite clearly on a good echo-sounder.

What you are likely to see

Besides the boilers, bollards, steel plates and ribs, some complete sections are scattered amongst the reef. At the bow, which lies to the south of the boilers, the remains of anchor winches and chain can be found. The stern is broken away and lies about 20m north. Today one can still find shell cases and numerous lead balls from the anti-personnel shell it was also carrying. Beware of touching any detonators, which are conical and made of brass. They may look harmless but can contain unstable explosives.

Velvet swimming crab

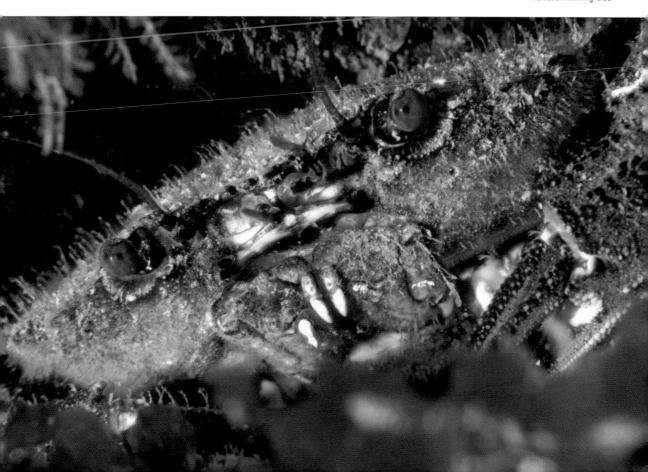

29

Twenty-nine

Porthkerris and Drawna Rock

Type Reef, shore and night
Level Novice diver **Depth** 0-25m

Air and dive shop Seaways, Cornish Diving, Haven Scuba, Dive Action and Porthkerris Divers.

Position Porthkerris Beach

Description

The cove provides excellent launch facilities and access to the famous Manacles reef just offshore, but also offers one of the best beach dives in Cornwall. Porthkerris Diving and Watersports own the site and can provide good facilities for the visiting diver. Access and parking on the beach are excellent and the sea is only a few metres from your car, so there are no long hikes with your kit. The cove nestles under high cliffs and is protected from all but east winds. So in the summer, when the prevailing south-westerly winds can be very strong, Porthkerris is generally flat and calm. The beach drops away quickly towards a fringing reef at the northern end of the cove that breaks the surface no more than 100m offshore, even at high water. Behind these visible rocks a submerged reef arcs out for a further 200m or so, accessing depths of 20-25m depending on the state of the tide. You can explore everything from shallow inshore reefs to deeper waters all within a 300m swim.

Cuttlefish eggs on gorgonian coral

How/when to dive

The dive is good at any state of the tide, but be cautious of the stronger north-east/south-west currents on the seaward side of the reef during periods of spring tides – either stay inshore or time your dive for slack water. The northern end of the beach has a path down the rocks with a rope handrail to help negotiate the steepest part. Enter the water next to a group of rocks close to the edge (these rocks dry at low water) and opposite the largest of the surface-breaking rocks, perhaps 100m offshore. Swim on the surface to the north-western edge of the offshore rocks. From the large rock edge, dive and swim east and seaward, with the reef on your right shoulder. The sea bed here is made up of heavy granite pebbles and shingle, so the visibility is often very good. As you follow the reef

the depth increases rapidly from 6m to 12-15m, depending on the tide. The reef is then bisected by a number of cuts and gullies crying out to be explored, though your first dive is best spent familiarising yourself with the topography and routes for your return. Continuing seaward the big reef wall terminates on your right and you encounter some large individual rocks, which are the beginning of the reef running further out into deeper water. Here, again depending on the tide, you can either continue seaward on the low reef to deeper water and return the same way, or continue right along the seaward face of the reef. Along here is a section of wall, slightly undercut in places, that reaches 4-5m in height before the reef forms a series of steps and ledges

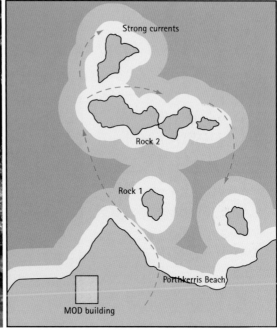

Cuckoo wrasse

towards the surface. Following this wall you come to the end of the first main block of reef, which becomes more broken, though no less massive. This area offers more gullies and undercuts to be explored, and you can happily work your way along until the reef begins to rise on your right towards the gully between rocks 1 and 2 (see map). Either follow the gully or continue around rock 2 towards the shore once more. From here you can either follow the patches of rock and reef on the sea bed on a compass bearing towards the shore (easiest if there is any tide) or surface and swim back. If you choose to follow the reef seaward, pick a slack water period and ensure that you have a good compass bearing for your return, and enough air.

The reef peters out in 25m or so on a dark, sandy sea floor where there is a healthy scallop bed. Even on a neap tide the current out here beyond the shelter of the headland can be quite strong, so be cautious and turn back with plenty of air. If you make the swim offshore, beware of boats from both the dive centre and visiting groups.

What you are likely to see

During the summer the shallow waters of Porthkerris are a favourite hunting ground for small shoals of large grey mullet, which can be seen darting through the seaweed forests. Below the kelp line reveals the rock face and its garlands of jewel anemones, tunicates, sea cucumbers and sponges. Don't ignore the sea bed as this is home to all sorts of bottom-dwelling fish, crustaceans, tube worms, anemones and in the spring and summer months, hordes of juvenile cuttlefish. On the deeper part of the dive the rock face is exposed to tidal current so it is covered with filter-feeding dead man's fingers, jewel anemones and sponges, making it quite colourful, especially in a torch beam. Further along the reef is home to several varieties of fish - marauding pollack, the occasional bass, ballan and corkwing wrasse, cheeky cuckoo wrasse that peer into your mask, and more unusual species such as red gurnard and John Dory.

Thirty

Porthoustock

Type Reef, shore and night
Level Novice diver **Depth** 5-15m

Air and dive shop Seaways,
Cornish Diving, Haven Scuba,
Dive Action and Porthkerris Divers.

Position Porthoustock Cove

Description

Porthoustock is mainly used as a launch site for the Manacles and the Lizard although you can shore dive here and some clubs use it for training.

How/when to dive

The centre of the cove is mostly dark so it is best to dive the sides of the cove which have reef systems with the usual shallow water critters – venturing too far out you will begin to feel the effects of the tide from the Manacles. There are minimal facilities although there is sometimes a burger caravan on busy bank holiday weekends.

What you are likely to see

The sandy area usually has quite a few flatties - especially at either end of the day on a high tide. The reefs at either side support an abundance of short-spined sea scorpions and snakelocks anemones. This is often used for training with more experienced divers venturing out to the Manacles.

The Manacles

The Manacles reef is a hugely popular dive site and the next four dives are some of the best. The reason is that they have an abundance of stunning marine life. Furthermore, due to their dangerous position for shipping they host an impressive number of wrecks. The chart opposite shows the general area and the close proximity of the dives to each other. The whole site is worthy of exploring so if you are adventurous pick a spot and dive it! Of all the regions

around the UK that I have dived and know about, the Manacles must be in the top ten. Unfortunately the Manacles can be a dangerous place to dive at times. The strong tide that supports the great variety of marine life can be ferocious, especially on springs. In the past many clubs have used the area as the traditional Easter dive site – for many the first dive of the season. By default, at this time of the lunar cycle there will be a spring tide. It claims a fatality most years. Moreover,

Plumose anemone

the Manacles are very exposed to sudden changes in the weather and offer no shelter to any element of an easterly wind. That said, thousands of fantastic dives are safely carried out each season. Observe the tide, seek local knowledge, get a shipping forecast and make one of them.

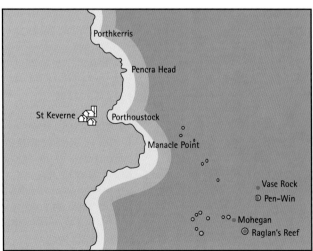

Porthkerris

Pencra Head

St Keverne

Porthoustock

Manacle Point

Vase Rock

Pen-Win

Mohegan

Raglan's Reef

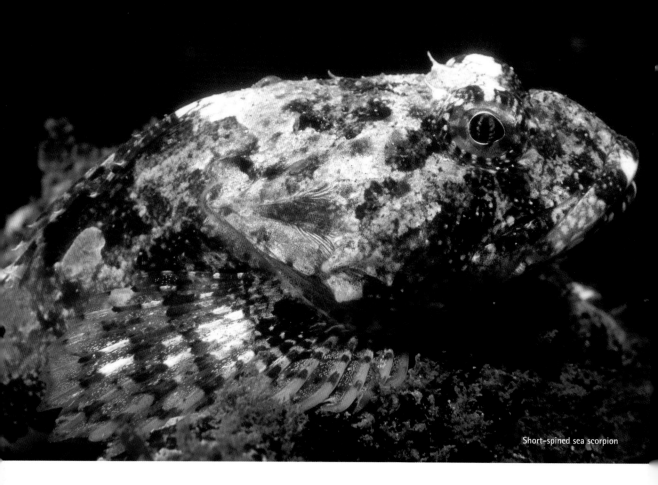
Short-spined sea scorpion

31

Thirty-one

Vase Rock

Type Reef **Level** Sport diver
Depth 8-45m

Launch St Mawes, St Just, Falmouth, Mylor, Mawnan Smith, Porthkerris and Porthoustock.
Air and dive shop Seaways , Cornish Diving, Haven Scuba, Dive Action, Porthkerris Divers and Sea Acres.

Position 50°02.874'N
005°002.410'W

Description

This spectacular submerged rock is definitely worth a visit. It is difficult to find without accurate GPS marks and a good echo-sounder. The highest point is about 5m below the surface but in calm weather and good visibility it is quite easy to spot from the surface. Be aware Vase rocks breaks the surface at low water spring tide.

How/when to dive

It must be dived at slack water, as the currents around the Manacles can be strong. Slack is four and a half hours before high water Falmouth. There is another small slack period one to two hours after high water which can be used on neap tides.

What you are likely to see

On the seaward side this stunning pinnacle is almost completely covered in jewel anemones in an amazing array of colours. Towards the leeward side of the rock dead man's fingers and massive clumps of hydroids prevail. Dogfish and anglerfish use this site for breeding in the spring months. The top 12m support a massively thick kelp forest which is a safe haven for numerous wrasse and makes an ideal decompression stop or advanced training area. The bottom is approximately 45m although most of the profusion of life is above 25m. Visibility is usually very good at around 10-15m although in spring and late summer it can be in excess of 25m.

32

Thirty-two

Pen-win

Type Reef **Level** Sport diver
Depth 5-42m

Launch St Mawes, St Just, Falmouth, Mylor, Mawnan Smith, Porthkerris and Porthoustock.
Air and dive shop Seaways, Cornish Diving, Haven Scuba, Dive Action, Porthkerris Divers and Sea Acres.

Position 50°02.855'N
005°002.030'W

Description

Pen-win rock lies about 8m beneath the surface and is a sheer wall that decends to 32m. It is relatively easy to find because if there is any swell a disturbance can be seen on the surface of the water. It is similar in underwater terrain to Vase Rock to which it is joined by 30m saddle.

How/when to dive

See Vase Rock (Dive 31).

What you are likely to see

The spectacular sea mount hosts a huge variety of marine life. Underwater it comprises a series of ledges, steep walls, gullies and deep crevices that cover a large area rather than a single pinnacle like Vase Rock. In early spring at around 20m Pen-win sometimes plays host to large numbers of breeding dogfish. One year there were females every couple of metres or so around its circumference. Below 30m on the deeper ledges huge anglerfish can sometimes be found – the biggest I have seen being around 1.5m long. Later in the summer months there are often huge shoals of mackerel and whiting. To the east and in deeper water there is evidence of wreckage including the rudder of the Mohegan.

Ling

Free-swimming conger eel

Thirty-three

The Mohegan

Type Wreck **Level** Sport diver
Depth 17-28m

Launch St Mawes, St Just, Falmouth, Mylor, Mawnan Smith, Porthkerris and Porthoustock.

Air and dive shop Seaways, Cornish Diving, Haven Scuba, Dive Action, Porthkerris Divers and Sea Acres.

Position 50°02.715'N
005°02.590'W

Description

The Mohegan was a 482ft, 6,889 gross tonnage luxury, four-masted, single-funnel liner. She sank in mysterious circumstances after hitting the Manacles reef on 14 October 1898 with the loss of all her crew, although the local lifeboat did manage to save the lives of quite a few passengers. The wreck is rumoured to be haunted, which may account for the abnormally large amount of divers who have lost their lives diving it!

How/when to dive

The Mohegan needs to be dived at slack water which is one to two hours before low water Falmouth. On weak neap tides it can be dived at most states of the tide. The best way to locate its boilers is to use the transits below and an echo-sounder. They are about 50m north-east of Maen Voes.

What you are likely to see

The wreckage starts in about 16m of water continuing downwards until its four boilers that sit in about 26m.

An abundance of fish life is usually shoaling around its superstructure. Good visibility is quite common in early spring so most of the hull can be seen at one time. Some of the holds are littered with floor tiles and crockery bearing the name and crest of the shipping line 'Thomas Wilson Sons and Co. Ltd, Hull' and a few luxury artefacts belonging to the passengers are still found each year. Spend some time peering into all the crevices and holes as large conger eels litter the wreck.

Plumose anemones

Kitting-up on a RIB

Transit points

If you are approaching the Mohegan by RIB or hard boat and have no GPS to guide you, here are some useful transit marks to help locate the wreck.

Transit B
Porthoustock
Manacle Point
Mohegan
Transit A

Transit A
Trees
Lowland Point

Transit B
Concrete block

34
Thirty-four

Raglan's Reef

Type Reef **Level** Sport diver
Depth 5-40m

Launch St Mawes, St Just, Falmouth, Mylor, Mawnan Smith, Porthkerris and Porthoustock.
Air and dive shop Seaways, Cornish Diving, Haven Scuba, Dive Action, Porthkerris Divers and Sea Acres.

Position 50°02.665'N
          005°02.523'W

Description

This is the most seaward of a series of reefs and looks very impressive on the echo-sounder, rising sheer from a depth of 45-50m, like a church spire, to within 3-4m of the surface.

How/when to dive

It must be dived at slack water, which is four hours before high water Falmouth and one to two hours after. On good neap tides it can be dived any time except on the full flood or ebb tide. Finding Raglan's Reef could not be simpler. Start about 400m inshore of the east cardinal buoy at Pen-win (refer to Admiralty Chart 777) then travel due south in about 45m of water until you find the last three southerly seaward rocks of the Manacles. Stay on this course until you observe a large, prominent house with a chimney breast to either side, virtually due west. Arrange for the house to 'sit' above the middle of the three rocks and head inshore on this transit. When the

echo-sounder quickly rises to about 5m that is the start of the reef. The reef then runs roughly due west inshore. Note: drive extremely slowly around the reef as slightly to the north there are some rocks which lie just below the surface at low tide.

What you are likely to see

The north-east side of this pinnacle is a series of vertical rock faces, which are carpeted with plumose anemones in a variety of colours. Just below the kelp line at around 8m the rocks are covered with hydroids, masses of brittle stars, endless arrays of jewel anemones and soft corals. This is an excellent site for photography, not least because of the range of subjects, but also because of the depth ranges available in one dive. You can start off in deep waters which have ling, dogfish, John Dory, striped mullet and anglerfish lying on the many ledges. The shallow is a perfect place to decompress. Early in the year it is quite common to see the giant jellyfish *Rhizostoma pulmo* that grows to more than a metre in diameter. The site is especially exhilarating when there is some tide running, as you will often encounter shoals of mullet or pollack sheltering from the current in the lee of the rock, occasionally darting out to feed. Even the odd bass is not uncommon. Raglan's Reef should only be attempted with an experienced boatman who can drop you at the right time and will know where to pick you up.

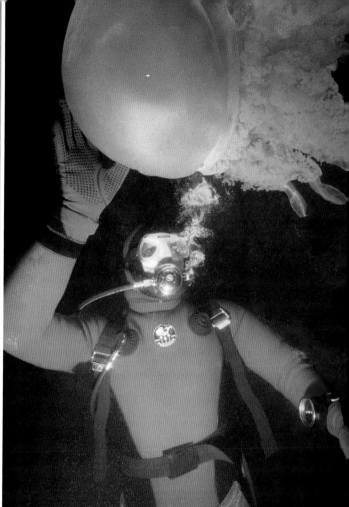

Diver with Rhizostoma jellyfish

Thirty-five

SS Carmarthen

Type Wreck **Level** Sport diver
Depth 20m

Launch St Mawes, St Just, Falmouth, Mylor, Mawnan Smith, Porthkerris and Porthoustock.
Air and dive shop Seaways, Cornish Diving, Haven Scuba, Dive Action, Porthkerris Divers and Sea Acres.

Position 50°00.117'N
005°07.451'W

Description

The Carmarthen was an armed steamship 380ft-long weighing 4,265 gross tons. She was torpedoed on 26 July 1917 by the German submarine UB-50 and sank with confidential papers and code-books still on board. The wreck was quite heavily salvaged some 50 years later and is quite broken-up except for its boilers.

How/when to dive

Offshore from Kennack Sands lie two large rocks known locally as Asparagus Island and Gull Rock. Wreckage can be found all around this area but the best dive sites are under the cliffs to the south of the cove towards Lion Rock. Average depths are slightly shallower at 10-15m and the topography consists of deep gullies. The whole area can be dived at all states of the tide on neaps tides or between high water Falmouth and 3 hours after high water on a spring tide.

What you are likely to see

All the normal shallow water marine life is found here and you have a good chance of encountering groups of cuttlefish in the summer months. The Camarthen initially had four boilers but generally only three can be found rising some 4m from the sea bed. Visibility is often very good here due to the bright, heavy, granite-sand sea bed. It is also an ideal site for more experienced novices and advanced training.

Spiny starfish

Thirty-six

Vrogue Rock and The Czar

Type Wreck and reef **Level** Sport diver
Depth 10-18m

Launch St Mawes, St Just, Mylor, Falmouth, Mawnan Smith, Porthkerris and Porthoustock.
Air and dive shop Seaways, Cornish Diving, Haven Scuba, Dive Action, Porthkerris Divers and Sea Acres.

Position 49°57.551'N
005°10.417'W

Description

This 1,100-ton iron barque-rigged screw steamer hit Vrogue Rock on 22 January 1859. She carried over 1,500 tons of government stores including cannon, shot, shell, uniform, clothing, hides, spirits, oil, sugar and cinnamon. After boiler trouble she tried to reach Falmouth in rough seas but hit the rock and fell broadside badly holed. She broke in two and quickly sank.

How/when to dive

Vrogue Rock lies just 2m below the surface and the water swirls around it on the flood and ebb tide. Diving should therefore be carried out on slack water which is about four and a half hours before high water Devonport.

What you are likely to see

The Czar lies fairly broken-up in 10-18m of water just to the north-east of Vrogue Rock. There are several massive 68-pounder shots, which are about 18cm in diameter, strewn over the wreckage. Some of the huge guns for which they were intended, are found here too. When diving her it is worth searching carefully in cracks and gullies in the rocks, where military buttons, buckles and badges from the uniforms in its cargo are often found. Many of the gullies are full of musket shot while conger, ling and the occasional lobster can be found under the plates. Pouting, goldsinney and whiting often shoal in small numbers over the broken ship's superstructure.

Ling and conger eel

Jewel anemones

37

Thirty-seven

Hot Point, Bass Point and Lizard Point

Type Reef and wreck **Level** Sport diver
Depth 10-16m

Description

The whole area around the southern tip of the Lizard is littered with countless wrecks. The Adolf Vinnen was a 262ft-long, 1,840-ton diesel-powered steel vessel that now lies in two halves with her engines about the only identifiable remains. She foundered on 23 February 1923 just 70m from the cliffs. Slightly more offshore are the remains of the Clan Malcolm, a 5,743-ton steamship. She sank in thick fog on 26 September 1935 with all her crew surviving. The smallest of the wrecks listed was Le Vieux Tigre at 260 tons, who also succumbed to fog and sank on 27 March 1935. Both her remains and the wreckage of the Mosel are difficult to distinguish from one another. The Mosel was a 3,201-ton barquentine-rigged German steamship which ran aground – again in thick fog – on 9 August 1882. Yet again in fog, the magnificent sailing vessel Cromdale ran aground on 23 May 1913. The Queen Margaret was a four-masted steel barque that ran aground on Maenheere Rock with her cargo of wheat on 5 May 1913. The iron steamship Suffolk was some 2,924 tons and 303ft-long. She ran aground in

thick fog on 28 September 1886 with her cargo of wheat and flour. Sadly most of her livestock were drowned but all the crew survived.

How and when to dive

All the wrecks and surrounding area must be dived on a neap tide and low water slack which is approximately four and a half hours before high water Devonport. Lizard Point experiences very strong currents – sometimes in excess of 5 knots – so great care should be taken. The surrounding sea is also prone to heavy ground swell and diving should only be considered on the calmest of days.

What you are likely to see

The list given is of some of the larger or more intact vessels that sank in the area. However, all of them are heavily broken-up and diving them is more of a rummage in an underwater scrap-yard rather than on a specific wreck. The general underwater terrain consists of rocky gullies with superb macro life and wrasse, bass, pollack and mackerel are all common in the summer months.

Launch St Mawes, St Just, Mylor, Falmouth, Mawnan Smith, Portkerris and Porthhoustock.
Air and dive shop Seaways, Cornish Diving, Haven Scuba, Dive Action, Porthkerris Divers and Sea Acres.

Positions

Adolf Vinnen	49°57.887'N 005°11.018'W
Clan Malcolm	49°57.825'N 005°10.840'W
Le Vieux Tigre	49°57.790'N 005°11.008'W
Mosel	49°57.780'N 005°11.090'W
Cromdale	49°57.705'N 005°11.179'W
Queen Margaret	49°57.940'N 005°12.330'W
Suffolk	49°57.680'N 005°12.830'W

Nudibranchs

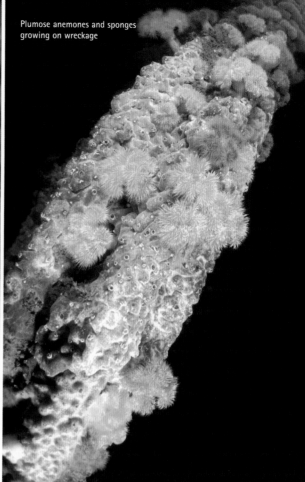
Plumose anemones and sponges growing on wreckage

38
Thirty-eight

Mullion Island

Type Reef **Level** Sport diver
Depth 8-25m

Launch Porthleven, Marazion
and Penzance.
Air and dive shop Trevair, Undersea
Adventures and Mount's Bay Diving.

Position 50°00.700'N
005°15.960'W

Description

Mullion is a small fishing village on the south-west side of the Lizard Peninsula close to the town of Helston. Less than half a mile offshore from Mullion Harbour lies the large rocky outcrop of Mullion Island.

How/when to dive

The leeward side of the island offers some interesting gully diving in 8-15m of water. However, much more spectacular diving can be found 200m to the west on the seaward side of the island. Here the reef starts at 16-18m and drops sharply to 25m in the deeper gullies. Tides are not a great problem except during springs when diving should be planned for slack water - especially on the seaward side - which is four and a half hours after or one and a half hours before high water Penzance.

What you are likely to see

On the inside of the island the odd seal or diving sea bird from the large colonies on the rock are known to visit divers. Keep an eye out for a collection of iron cannons in a deep gully on the south-western corner of the island, the origin of which is still a mystery. The outer reefs support outcrops of the attractive Ross coral and gorgonians and in the spring you will find a profusion of reproducing nudibranchs.

Diver explores the John R Park

39

Thirty-nine

The John R Park

Type Wreck **Level** Advanced diver
Depth 40-55m

Launch Porthleven, Marazion
and Penzance.
Air and dive shop Trevair, Undersea
Adventures and Mount's Bay Diving.

Position 49°59.899N
005°24.647'W and
50°00.067'N
005°24.583'W

Description

The John R Park was a 441ft-long, 7,184 gross ton American Liberty ship similar to the James Eagan Layne (see dive 4). She was torpedoed by U-399 (Buhse) on 21 March 1945. Although extensively damaged she did not go down immediately, giving enough time for her to be abandoned. Her captain, Otto L Bartfeld, even re-boarded to see if she could be salvaged but there was no hope. Some six hours after being hit she broke in two and sank.

How/when to dive

Slack water on the John R Park is two and a half hours before or after high water at Devonport.

What you are likely to see

The wreck is fairly intact and rises 15m or so off the sea bed. It is in two distinct parts and it is possible to penetrate the bridge section and wheel-house but the roof has started to collapse. Towards the bow there are still a few shell cases on the sea bed. Large anemones cover the hull and huge pollack seek shelter in its superstructure. There are several enormous conger eels under some of its plates, as well as some rust-coloured lobsters. Less than 200m away lies the wreck of what might be the Vigrid, at position 49°59.933'N 005° 24.550'W.

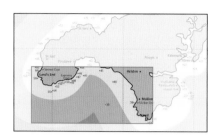

3

West towards Land's End

Land's End is a part of Cornwall better known to sightseers than to divers. En route to the most
western tip of England you pass the famous Minack Theatre – an open air stage cut into the
face of the cliffs at Porthcurno – but the drama continues under the surface of the sea. The
rugged granite topography of the peninsula extends well out to sea – Wolf Rock some 11 miles
offshore gives an indication of just how far it continues. Particular to this part of Cornwall is the
colour of the cliffs and sea. The sun sets over the open ocean with no land or pollution to diffract
its light, resulting in a warm iridescent glow that can last long after the sun itself has disappeared
behind the horizon. On a clear day one can clearly make out the Isles of Scilly about 24 miles to
the west. Almost every cove has some legend originating from either the bygone smuggling days
or the many famous shipwrecks who foundered on the rocks, and mythical stones like the Merry
Maidens tell us of secret rituals from centuries past.

Beneath the waves the water is clean – free from river estuaries and with the undissolving
granite rock, there is little to cloud the visibility except for the plankton in spring. The plankton,
however, is not unwelcome as with it comes the majestic basking shark. I have seen more than
30 in a single day between Lamorna Cove and the Runnelstone. There are carpets of anemones
on the exposed surfaces of the submerged rocks. There is one such wall just west from the City of
Westminster wreck. It is about 50m long with no rock visible due to the sheer density of marine life.
This section also contains the landmark that many a seaman welcomes from a safe distance – the
Longships Lighthouse. Besides guiding ships around the perilous coast, it also marks the best reef
dive with aquatic life in an abundance to rival any tropical reef. For the diver there is also a great
sense of interaction with the wildlife – it has been known for pods of dolphins to shadow local
RIBs for more than an hour at a time.

Longships Lighthouse

Sunset at Sennen

Forty

Great Row

Type Reef **Level** Sport diver
Depth 14-25m

Launch Porthleven,
Marazion and Penzance.
Air and dive shop Trevair, Undersea
Adventures and Mount's Bay Diving.

Position 50°03.990'N
005°23.500'W

Description

This site is approximately two and a half
miles west of Porthleven, and consists of
a large area of reef with a plateau at 10-
12m which drops off to 25-30m.

How/when to dive

The area is exposed to the full force
of the tide and is consequently a slack
water dive - four and a half hours after
or one and a half hours before high
water Penzance. The best diving is to be
found to the south-east of the plateau.

What you are likely to see

You will find lush marine growth on
the exposed rock faces with sponges,
Ross coral and gorgonian sea fans. The
reef also attracts shoals of mackerel
and bass, while the sandy sea bed
surrounding the area is home to large
flatfish and scallops.

Whiting

41

Forty-one

Prussia Cove

Type Reef and wreck
Level Novice diver **Depth** 5-15m

Launch Porthleven,
Marazion and Penzance.
Air and dive shop Trevair, Undersea
Adventures and Mount's Bay Diving.

Position 49°57.550'N
005°10.417'W

Description

Prussia Cove can be found on the eastern side of Mount's Bay behind Cudden Point. Along with Bessy's Cove to the east they are famous for their smuggling history. For the diver they offer sheltered diving suitable for all levels. There is also a large rock island just outside the cove to the north-east which has a long tunnel passing through it and makes a great dive for an 'advanced novice' or a second dive.

How/when to dive

The most attractive area is found on the eastern side of the cove where the low cliffs plunge into the sea. This area is riddled with deep gullies, swim-throughs and some spectacular tunnels full of life, where many happy hours can be spent without referring to your computer or tables. Just off the eastern arm of the cove stands a rock called the Enys. It is between here and a point perhaps 50m off the beach that the best diving can be found. The spurs and gullies seen on the foreshore are reflected in the underwater topography

as they meander in all directions. Average depths are 6-12m and the site is totally sheltered from tidal streams. In the centre of Prussia Cove is found the wreckage of the stranding of HMS Warspite in 1947 while under tow to the breakers' yard.

What you are likely to see

The general topography is made from a series of gullies, tunnels and ledges. The kelp can be quite thick in the summer but provides a perfect refuge for juvenile marine life. On a few dives I have seen free-swimming conger eels, obviously used to the presence of divers. The rock faces of the gullies are carpeted with life - some of which is quite unusual or rare. Sponges of all sorts compete for space with sea squirts, both the attractive light bulb variety and the carpeting strawberry tunicate. Add to this the colonies of colourful anemones and there is so much colour that when the water is clear you find yourself comparing

Dover sole

it to the tropics: jewel, daisy, dahlia, strawberry, beadlet and snakelocks all decorate this underwater garden. There is a seal colony nearby on Cudden Point and you will often find them around or on the rock island. To the western side of the island you will find the spectacular tunnel, some 25-30m in length, which runs through the corner of the island. As you enter the tunnel you cannot quite see the exit due to a bend but after 10m or so the light appears. This large tunnel is wide enough for two divers and the

occasional seal! The roof is carpeted with red and orange sea squirts and a variety of colourful anemones so you should take a torch. The tunnel is safe in calm conditions but should be avoided if a swell prevails as depths are only 6-10m and the surge can be quite remarkable. In the open waters just out of the gullies you will find shoals of sand eels, mullet and juvenile mackerel and packs of hunting pollack. In July and August when plankton can be heavier and calm, glassy seas are more frequent, it is not

unknown to see basking sharks taking a turn through the cove, scooping the microscopic food down their cavernous throats. Another, perhaps rarer visitor at this time of year is the Atlantic trigger-fish, which is seen all along this coast as far as Plymouth, and can be quite a surprise when found standing its ground at the end of a gully.

John Dory

42
Forty-two

The Warspite

Type Wreck **Level** Novice diver
Depth 9m

Launch Porthleven,
Marazion and Penzance.
Air and dive shop Trevair, Undersea
Adventures and Mount's Bay Diving.

Position 50°07.083'N
005°28.850'W

Description
The Warspite was a 640ft battleship which broke her tow to the breakers' yard in 1947. She first sank at Prussia Cove but was refloated and towed to St Michael's Mount, where over the following three years she was cut up for scrap.

How/when to dive
The wreck can be dived at any state of the tide.

What you are likely to see
Her two large boilers remain on the sea bed at about 8m while among the reef there are plenty of large plates, sometimes moved by heavy storms. Congers and blennies are permanent residents in the boiler tubes and in the spring numerous species of nudibranchs congregate on the broken superstructure to breed. It is also possible to spot squid here.

Forty-three

The Alice Marie

Type Wreck **Level** Sport diver
Depth 25m

Launch Porthleven,
Marazion and Penzance.
Air and dive shop Trevair, Undersea
Adventures and Mount's Bay Diving.

Position 50°06.141'N
005°29.412-498'W

Description
This 277ft, 2,181 gross tonnage French steel barque sunk on 4 October 1908 after being holed on the Runnelstone in thick fog. She was making for the shallow water of St Michael's Mount but sank before she could ground herself.

How/when to dive
You can dive the wreck at any state of the tide and she is often buoyed in the summer months.

What you are likely to see
She was heavily salvaged in the mid-1980s but there are plenty of plates which are covered in dead man's fingers and plumose anemones. Fish life can be quite abundant - there are one or two huge conger eels living under the steel ribs and John Dory are quite common in the summer months. The surrounding waters are not the clearest so she is best dived after a period of calm weather and on a flooding tide.

Nudibranch

44

Forty-four

Low Lee Ledges and The Primrose

Type Reef **Level** Sport diver
Depth 5-22m

Launch Porthleven, Marazion, Penzance and Lamorna Cove.
Air and dive shop Trevair, Undersea Adventures and Mount's Bay Diving.

Position 50°05.440'N
005°31.400'W

Description

The north-facing, moon-shaped reef is marked at the north-east tip by an east cardinal buoy. Penzance BSAC have established a nature trail here which you can follow from the wreck of the Primrose (which is buoyed in the summer). The Primrose was carrying a cargo of coal when she struck Low Lee Ledges on 23 August 1906. She sat there for a month before bad weather eventually broke her back and she sank.

How/when to dive

The area can be dived at all tidal states.

What you are likely to see

Dead man's fingers, goldsinney, wrasse and lots of cuttlefish can usually be seen throughout the summer. The depth ranges from 5m at the top of the rocks to 22m north of the wreck. On the north and east side lie two iron cannons from an unknown Dutch East Indiaman. The Primrose is well broken-up but her ribs are clearly visible and there are plenty of shoals of bib and other juvenile fish to look out for.

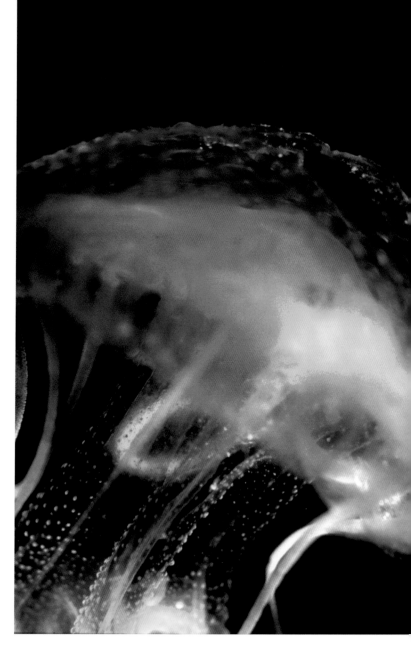

Juvenile jellyfish

Plumose anemone

45
Forty-five

The Hellopes

Type Wreck **Level** Advanced diver
Depth 28-34m

Launch Porthleven, Marazion,
Penzance and Lamorna Cove.
Air and dive shop Trevair, Undersea
Adventures and Mount's Bay Diving.

Position 50°04.563'N
005°29.595'W

Description

This 320ft-long, 2,774 gross ton coal-laden steamship sank on 21 December 1911. She sprang a leak off Land's End in a gale on her last intended voyage before being scrapped. By the time she had navigated past Mousehole her pumps where unable to stop the rising water and she sank. She now lies in three parts on her starboard side.

How/when to dive

Although diveable at nearly all states of the tide you should avoid spring tides.

What you are likely to see

Often buoyed during the summer months, Hellopes lies north-west to south-east with her stern lying on its starboard side. The most impressive part of this wreck is the large steel propeller and rudder. Just forward of her midships there are two enormous boilers which stand upright at about 5m. Her bow, which is fairly apparent due to the large amount of chain found there, is covered in sea fans and set at an angle with both masts lying to one side. You will also find much of her superstructure is covered in fantastic plumose anemones.

Edible sea–urchin

46
Forty-six

The Conqueror

Type Wreck **Level** Advanced diver
Depth 28-34m

Launch Porthleven, Marazion,
Penzance and Lamorna Cove.
Air and dive shop Trevair, Undersea
Adventures and Mount's Bay Diving.

Position 50°04.349'N
005°32.412'W

Description
The Conqueror was a 1,157-ton trawler
that ran aground on 26 December 1977
in perfectly calm weather. Her mate
was reportedly held responsible for
leaving the bridge unattended while he
went below for breakfast. Drifting on
automatic pilot she ran aground just off
Penzer Point.

How/when to dive
The wreck can be dived at any state of
the tide.

What you are likely to see
She has broken into three distinct parts.
Although a relatively recent wreck, over
the past 25 years marine life has built
up and covers the majority of her plates.
This dive makes a good training site for
novices who already have some open
water experience.

Edible crab hides in a wreck

47

Forty-seven

The Ansgir

Type Wreck and reef **Level** Novice diver
Depth 7-15m

Launch Marazion, Penzance
and Lamorna Cove.
Air and dive shop Trevair, Undersea
Adventures and Mount's Bay Diving.

Position 50°04.080'N
005°32.644'W

Description

Further along the coast from the Conqueror and slightly west of Penzer Point is the wreck site of the Ansgir. At 438ft and some 6,500 tons this was one of the largest ships ever wrecked off the Cornish coast. She was handed over to Britain by Germany in part payment after World War I. En route to Barry from France she struck the rocks off Penzer Point and became a total loss on 1 December 1920.

How/when to dive

The Ansgir can be dived at any state of the tide.

What you are likely to see

The only recognisable parts are her boilers, which can be found close to the shore near a rock shaped like a shark fin at a depth of about 7-10m. Her plates and wreckage are scattered over a large area. Towards Penzer Point itself there are some nice gullies going down to around 15m that provide a home for juvenile fish in the summer months. This is also a good training dive but is prone to swell in relatively small seas.

48
Forty-eight
Lamorna Cove

Type Reef and shore **Level** Novice diver
Depth 9m

Air and dive shop Trevair, Undersea
Adventures and Mount's Bay Diving.

Position Lamorna Cove

Description

This is a shallow, sheltered cove with a
sandy sea bed surrounded by a rocky,
reef shoreline. There is good parking,
a café and WC and a good slip for
launching RIBs (a four-wheel drive
vehicle is advisable). This makes an ideal
site for training dives, the first dive of
the season and night diving.

How/when to dive

The cove can be dived at all states of
the tide but it can get quite shallow
on low water springs. Avoid diving
and launching when there is a southeasterly wind as the swell can produce
a surf of 2-3m within minutes. The
best night diving can be found one to
two hours before high water around a
full moon. Lamorna can be quite busy
with boat launching especially at bank
holiday weekends. It is advisable to
carry an SMB so local boat traffic can
see you easily. Note that due to the
profusion of weever fish at Lamorna it
is recommended to wear gloves at all

times. Snorkellers and bathers should
always wear something on their feet.

What you are likely to see

During the day the sand is deserted
except for the odd sand eel and
weever fish. The rocky reef either side
hides a host of small invertebrates,
sea scorpions, dahlia, beadlet and
snakelocks anemones. In the summer
months small cuttlefish and wrasse are
commonly found hiding in the kelp and
among the boulders. But it is night when
the cove really comes to life: the sandy
bottom is transformed into a frenzied
activity of pollack and whiting stalking
sand eels . Similar to lionfish in the Red
Sea the hunters dart in and out of your
torch beam that has illuminated their
prey. Flatfish of numerous species are
plentiful including dover sole, megrim,
plaice, flounder and brill. In the very
shallow water of the harbour look out
for iridescent squid that hunt in shoals
of twenty or so in late summer.

Cup coral

File shell

Loading a RIB

Above and right: Basking shark

49

Forty-nine

The Stannock

Type Reef and drift **Level** Sport diver
Depth 15-34m

Launch Penzance and Lamorna Cove.
Air and dive shop Trevair, Undersea
Adventures and Mount's Bay Diving.

Position 50°03.150'N
005°33.600'W

Description

Just over half a mile due south of
Lamorna Cove this fairly deep reef
makes a great drift dive when the tide
is running.

How/when to dive

Dive off slack water (see The Bucks)
for a drift dive but the reef is quite
enjoyable with no current. Head due
south out from Lamorna for half a mile
and the echo-sounder will read about
12m. Keep on the same heading until
the drop-off is clearly visible and pick
your depth. The reef runs roughly east
to west. It is usually marked by lobster
pot buoys throughout the summer.

What you are likely to see

Most of the interesting marine life on
this dive is deeper than 20m. The ledges
of the reef hide a variety of marine life,
including quite a few crustaceans. It
appears to be a breeding ground for
spider crabs and even crayfish, although
they are generally quite small. In deeper
water Ross coral is very common and in
excellent condition. At around 33m the
rocky sea bed gives way to sandy gullies
where anglerfish can usually be found.

Fifty

The Bucks

Type Reef **Level** Sport diver
Depth 5-36m

Launch Penzance and Lamorna Cove.
Air and dive shop Trevair, Undersea Adventures and Mount's Bay Diving.

Position 50°03.053'N
005°34.426'W

Description

The Bucks are two rocks connected by a reef system that shows at low water. They lie a few hundred metres offshore from the Tater Du lighthouse.

How/when to dive

The best diving is on the seaward side of the outer Buck with spectacular walls descending to 35m. Generally the Bucks can be dived at any state of the tide but on high springs it is advisable to dive on slack water. Slack is two hours before high water at Newlyn. Note that at high water they completely disappear under the water.

What you are likely to see

At about 9m there is a shaft that brings you out at about 22m. It is difficult to find but it is on the western side slightly to the south. Otherwise aim to dive below about 14m where the kelp gives way to large boulders. These have a good covering of jewel anemones and some very large cup corals. In late spring this is a favourite site to see male cuckoo wrasse in their full blue and orange mating colours. As interesting marine life can be found shallower than 20m this makes the site ideal for an array of training or build-up dives. Between the boulders and gullies at around 22m you will come across wreckage and coal from the two-masted, 215ft-long, 638-ton steamship the Garonne. She sank on 22 May 1868 due to a navigational error and is now very broken up. Towards the sea bed and below 28m there are some quite exquisite gorgonian sea fan corals and the rare red fingers. In mid-May when the plankton is usually at its thickest basking sharks are often seen - sometimes as many as 20 at a time.

51
Fifty-one

The Mystique

Type Wreck **Level** Sport diver
Depth 33m

Launch Penzance and Lamorna Cove.
Air and dive shop Trevair, Undersea Adventures and Mount's Bay Diving.

Position 50°03.013'N
005°34.716'W

Description
The Mystique was a 65ft wooden-hulled fishing vessel. Only a few years ago she mysteriously hit the outer Buck off Tater Du light in near-perfect conditions. She sank quickly but without loss of life. The wreck is virtually intact, listing to port on a sand and rock sea bed. Recently its hold started to split but it is still recognisable as an intact wreck.

How/when to dive
The Mystique can be dived at most states of the tide on neaps and at slack on springs, which is two hours before high water Newlyn. It is usually buoyed in the summer months as it can be difficult to find.

What you are likely to see
It is still covered in nets so a great deal of care is needed. Not much life has colonised it yet although quite a few crabs continue to get entangled in its nets. It will not take you long to dive the wreck and if you then head north for 20-30m you come to the start of a reef which climbs to within 7-8m of the surface. To the west side there are many gullies with plenty of marine life, making an excellent multilevel dive.

Diver and nets on the Mystique

Red mullet

Fifty-two

The Lincoln

Type Wreck **Level** Sport diver
Depth 32m

Launch Penzance and Lamorna Cove.
Air and dive shop Trevair, Undersea
Adventures and Mount's Bay Diving.

Position 50°02.793'N
005°35.600'W

Description

The Lincoln was a three-masted, schooner-rigged cargo steamship. Her bridge was amidships and the engine in her stern, in common with the majority of conversions from sail to steam power that took place at the time. She was 198ft-long with a gross tonnage of 624 tons. She sank on 5 July 1886 after hitting the Runnelstone in thick fog.

How/when to dive

Tides are not normally a problem on the Lincoln as it is protected by the headlands of Boscawen Point and Merthen Point to east and west. However, during high spring tides slack is about two hours before high water Newlyn. She is quite difficult to find but is often buoyed throughout the summer.

What you are likely to see

The hull is still recognisable although collapsed on one side, and the whole ship can easily be covered in one dive with a gentle depth range of 22-24m at the bow and 31-32m at the stern, depending on the tide. The site often offers excellent visibility and you will find the spare steel propeller on the bows and the remains of the wheelhouse, accommodation and funnel can be made out. The engine stands proud from the wreckage while the masts and spars lie out to the seaward side of the wreck. There are numerous hardwood sheaves, pulleys and other rigging equipment to be found. Her plates are home to a large variety of shoaling fish and marine life including some exceptional conger eels. Should you drift off the wreck the surrounding reef is a spectacular mixture of deep gullies and walls rich in marine life.

Fifty-three

Logan's Gully and Gull Rock

Type Reef **Level** Sport diver
Depth 5-30m

Launch Penzance and Lamorna Cove.
Air and dive shop Trevair, Undersea
Adventures and Mount's Bay Diving.

Position Gull Rock
 50°02.452'N
 005°37.984'W
 Outer rock
 50°02.348'N
 005°38.272'W

Porthcurno Bay and Logan's Rock

Description

This site is a superb spot for all levels of diving with the exception of complete novices. There are three different areas which, for the super-fit, can all be done in one dive. There is an anemone-encrusted gully with a shallow reef system, a steep wall dive and a third site consisting of a sand sea bed littered with large boulders.

How/when to dive

On springs any state of the tide except slack is required. The gully is found about 5m to the east of the outer rock. It has a depth of 15m on the seaward side, gently sloping upwards to about 9m inshore where there are numerous shallow reefs. To seaward and travelling

east the rocky reef meets the sand at about 22m. Continuing east there are spectacular walls running around Castle Treveen Point. Between Castle Treveen Point and Gull Rock the terrain is made up of huge boulders on a sandy bottom. The maximum depth here is about 28m although to the south it goes down to over 30m.

What you are likely to see

Logan's Gully is plastered with anemones of enormous variety. At the entrance it is common to find whiting and pollack stalking the resident shoals of sand eels. In the shallows many species of wrasse are common. In the summer blue trigger-fish - normally only seen in wamer climates - are often

sighted. Slightly to the west and inshore of the gully there is a small cave where a lobster lies - only half a metre high and just up from the sea bed. Further west and away from the rocks thornback rays and skate are common. Moving seaward cuttlefish hide where the rocks meet the sand so look for small, unusual indents in the sand. The rock face of Castle Treveen Point is covered in huge cup corals, sponges and jewel anemones. Nearer to Gull Rock there appears to be a favourite spawning ground for sea urchins - some years the rocks provide homes for hundreds of them. Cuckoo wrasse are ever-present, waiting for any tasty tit-bits the diver disturbs on the sea bed.

54
Fifty-four

Runnelstone

Type Reef **Level** Sport diver
Depth 12-38m

Launch Penzance,
Lamorna Cove and Sennen.
Air and dive shop Trevair, Undersea
Adventures and Mount's Bay Diving.

Position 50°01.351'N
005°40.340'W

Description

The Runnelstone is one of the most spectacular dive sites in the whole of Cornwall. It is covered by a prolific amount of marine life which is so thick in places that no rock face is visible. In addition there are countless ships that have foundered there, including the famous City of Westminster which literally knocked the top off the stone. Other wrecks include the Lake Grafton, Joshua Nicholson, Febrero and Moorview.

How/when to dive

Diving must be carried out at slack water which is about one and a half hours before high water Newlyn. On a spring tide it only lasts about 15 minutes so it is best to dive on neaps where slack usually at least an hour. There are several separate dives you can do at this site and the best recommendation is to explore different routes on each dive.

What you are likely to see

The rock starts at about 5m which is mainly covered in kelp. Below 15m the kelp gives way to huge rock walls covered in anemones – especially plumose anemones – which can be found in superb condition and in a vast array of colours. On the seaward side and towards 25m the wall tends to flatten out then drops again to around 36m. Here the sandy sea bed is broken by huge boulders more than 15m high. The sand is home to many large megrim, sole and flounder as well as the occasional gurnard. Between the boulders conger and ling are numerous and sometimes even occupy the same hole! Metal plates, anchors, chains and cables from the various wrecks can be found everywhere. The reef then continues seaward to a depth of about 48m. Inshore the sheerness of the face becomes less defined and a complex reef system extends for 100m or so towards the shore. The depth rises to 20-14m and here too there is plenty of evidence of wreckage on the sea bed. If the weather is calm, the better end to the dive is in the shallows at the top of the stone. Here at a depth of between 6-12m vast shoals of horse mackerel congregate. Also among the kelp-covered rock there are usually mullet shyly hiding. Here the rock is covered with jewel anemones, cup corals and many different varieties of *Sagartia* anemones. Alternatively heading north-west to position 50°01.456'N 005°40.350'W will bring you to plenty of wreckage in about 12-19m where shell cases are frequently found. At position 50°01.270'N 005°40.825'W there is a superb submerged pinnacle called Poldew. Its peak is at about 14m and it bottoms out at 25m to the north and 45m to the south. There is also wreckage here and the reef is particularly clean.

Top of the Runnelstone

Jewel anemones

Fifty-five

The City of Westminster

Type Wreck **Level** Sport diver
Depth 15-36m

Launch Penzance, Sennen
and Lamorna Cove.
Air and dive shop Trevair, Undersea
Adventures and Mount's Bay Diving.

Position 50°01.346'N
005°40.419'W

Description

The City of Westminster struck the Runnelstone on 8 October 1923 and knocked the top off the stone. The steamer was 470ft-long, weighed 6,094 gross tons and was travelling en route to Rotterdam from Belfast with a cargo of South African maize. She now lies at the south-west seaward side of the Runnelstone with the shallowest part beginning at 15m. The wreck follows the contours of the sea bed with her stern at 35m. Much wreckage can also be found on the sea bed nearby.

How/when to dive

To find the wreck with great accuracy start at the Runnelstone buoy in about 45m of water. Look to shore and line up the black and white marker with the red one on Gwennap Head. Drive on this bearing until the echo-sounder reads 10m and place the shot. The wreck will be about 10m south-west of the shot. A second check is to observe a white marker half way up Penberth cliff which becomes just obscured by Logan's Rock. Slack water is about one and a half hours before high tide at Newlyn and lasts about 60 minutes on a neap tide. It is difficult to dive on a spring tide as the slack is quite short and current too strong.

What you are likely to see

The wreck lies upright although quite broken-up. its starboard side is wedged against the Runnelstone and leads the way at the top to a well-known gully. The gully is covered with plumose anemones of amazing colours. Its stern section is the most intact part, its deepest point at about 36m. The large plates and superstructure shelter a variety of juvenile fish life and crustaceans. There are many different species of anemones and it is common to see crabs, lobster and huge conger eels. This is a good multilevel dive as decompression or safety stops can be carried out on the Runnelstone. While on the surface keep a watchful eye out for sunfish that are frequent visitors throughout the summer.

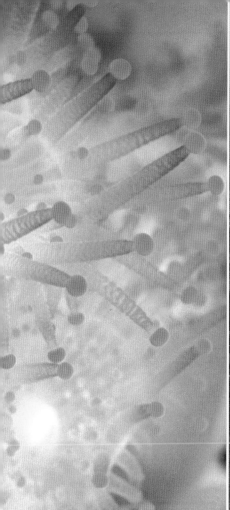

Diving on the City of Westminster

Fifty-six

Wolf Rock

Type Reef **Level** Sport diver
Depth 0-50m

Launch Penzance, Sennen
and Lamorna Cove.
Air and dive shop Trevair, Undersea
Adventures and Mount's Bay Diving.

Position 49°56.680'N
005°48.530'W

Description

Wolf Rock is a remote offshore rock approximately seven miles south-west of Gwennap Head. It is marked by an unmanned 34m-high lighthouse and therefore very easy to find.

How/when to dive

Diving can be done at any state of the tide, as even when there is a current you can dive on the lee side. However, if you want to be able to dive all around the rock, slack is at high water Newlyn on a neap tide. On springs there is no slack water.

What you are likely to see

The rock is basically a cone shape which slopes down at about 45 degrees to the sea bed 70m below the surface. It has the usual anemones found on the Runnelstone but they are not as prolific. Debris from building the lighthouse is scattered all around and is colonised by a variety of invertebrates. This site is good for deep dive training.

Diver, spider crab and
jewel anemones

Fifty-seven

Carn Base

Type Reef **Level** Sport diver
Depth 10-35m

Launch Penzance, Sennen
and Lamorna Cove.
Air and dive shop Trevair, Undersea
Adventures and Mount's Bay Diving.

Positions 50°01.907N
005°45.480W 17m
50°01.929N
005°45.507W 14m
50°01.937N
005°45.444W 10m

Description

Three pinnacles rise from depths of 35m to 14m covering a small area of about 100sqm: this area is known as Carn Base. Numerous ships have capsized in the surrounding waters, due to huge breaking swell that can occur in heavy weather. The current regularly exceeds 5 knots on a spring tide and marine life is prolific. I have a theory that where conditions make diving difficult, underwater life proliferates – and Carn Base is no exception to this theoretical rule. To the north, the strong tide of the Bristol Channel joins with the predominant tide of the English Channel and this mixing of currents supplies much food to the regular inhabitants. It really is a paradise for filter-feeders.

How/when to dive

The three main peaks of Carn Base range from 10-14m below the surface, falling to around 30m at the deepest point. Carn Base should be dived only on a neap tide at slack water, which starts about half an hour before high tide at Newlyn. Slack usually lasts for about an hour on neaps, and on springs you would not even notice it.

What you are likely to see

Between the huge numbers of sponges, anemones, sea squirts, brittle stars and starfish lie all kinds of crustaceans including crayfish, crabs and squat lobsters. And that's not all - there are huge shoals of mackerel, whiting and pollack, as well as occasional small shoals of silvery-grey mullet that dart in and out of the kelp. If the conditions are right, these can become prey to blue and porbeagle sharks. Due to the almost permanent current very little sediment settles, making it one of the healthiest sites in southern England.

Porthole on the
Torrey Canyon

Fifty-eight

Torrey Canyon

Type Wreck **Level** Sport diver
Depth 0-30m

Launch Penzance, Sennen
and Lamorna Cove.
Air and dive shop Trevair, Undersea
Adventures and Mount's Bay Diving.

Position Bow
50°03.669'N
006°08.267'W
Engine-room
50°02.456'N
006°07.657'W

Description

At the time the 974ft-long, 61,263-ton Liberian supertanker Torrey Canyon sank it was the largest tanker that had ever been built. It hit Pollard Rock on the Seven Stones reef on 18 March 1967 due to navigational error. It now lies well broken-up over an area of approximately one square mile, with the bow in a gully north-west of Pollard Rock and the stern over 300m to the south.

How/when to dive

Lying 17 miles west from Land's End the Torrey Canyon it is out of range of most RIBs. However, quite a few clubs venture there in perfect safety with a pair of well-equipped boats or on a hard boat. It is essential to get a detailed weather forecast before setting out. Diving the Torrey Canyon should be on slack water which starts approximately one hour before low water Newlyn. Due to the exposed position of the Seven Stones they should also only be dived in very calm conditions, as even when it is calm there is nearly always a large swell around the rocks. Note that most of the 'Stones' only break the surface on low water springs so take great care navigating the reef system.

What you are likely to see

The wreck is very broken-up due to the Navy blowing it up when they tried to burn off some of the oil it was carrying. There are plates scattered over a huge area but the bow is still relatively intact just north-west of Pollard Rock. As with many wrecks beware of any unexploded shells or bombs. The usual marine life can be found, as well as particularly large pollack. The surrounding reef is in excellent condition with huge amounts of red fingers, fan corals and jewel anemones. Like many of the offshore sites in Cornwall water visibility is exceptionally good.

59

Fifty-nine

Armed Knight

Type Reef **Level** Sport diver
Depth 16m

Launch Penzance, Sennen
and Lamorna Cove.
Air and dive shop Trevair, Undersea
Adventures and Mount's Bay Diving.

Position 50°03.716'N
005°42.960'W

Description
The Armed Knight is a rocky outcrop
about a quarter of a mile south of
Land's End.

How/when to dive
The area is prone to surge at any state
of the tide if the weather has recently
been stormy. The north-west tip is the
best area as it is quite a shallow and
ideal for novices who have some open
water experience.

What you are likely to see
The sea bed is a mixture of rocks, gullies
and boulders and the site is well-known
for its huge cup corals. Other marine
life includes lobster, edible crab, spider
crab and juvenile fish and although the
kelp can be quite thick in the summer
it is still an interesting dive. Numerous
bits of wreckage can be seen in the
gullies and occasionally coins and naval
artefacts are found.

Storm brewing over the Scilly Isles

Sixty

Longships

Type Reef **Level** Sport diver
Depth 12-45m

Launch Penzance,
Lamorna Cove and Sennen.
Air and dive shop Trevair, Undersea
Adventures and Mount's Bay Diving.

Position 50°03.980'N
005°44.785'W

Description

Arguably one of the best dives in the British Isles, the Longships reef is as dramatic underwater as it is above. Situated two miles west of Land's End a lighthouse marks the largest rock, below which there is complex reef system with a massive amount of invertebrate and fish life.

How/when to dive

On a spring tide it should only be dived at slack water which is about the same as high water Newlyn – you should avoid big tides. At neaps it can be dived virtually all the time except on the full flood or ebb. There are quite a few sites so if the current is running at one position it will generally be slack at the other sites. To make sure it is diveable, put a shot where you think it is slack and observe the buoy. It is a good idea to attach a 10m rope with a second large buoy on the end to the main shot – if you get your timing wrong the pull of the tide can completely submerge the main buoy. The most dramatic reef is a series of very deep gullies about 100m due west of the lighthouse. The gullies are easy to find with an echo-sounder - the first one drops from 12 to 34m, the second 15 to 36m and the third 20 to 54m. Further south the underwater topology is not as dramatic, but the diving is just as superb. If these two

Diver and edible crab

Sunfish

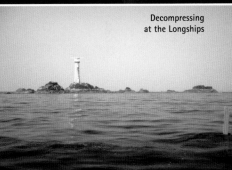

Decompressing
at the Longships

are not diveable due to a current then the third site is to the north of the lighthouse in a crescent-shaped inlet. Here the depth ranges from 14m to 30m depending on how far north you dive.

What you are likely to see

Stunning kelp-topped sheer walls are covered in a colourful spread of jewel anemones - the best in England. There is virtually every kind of anemone you will find in any identification book and at the bottom of the gullies huge rocks are home to lobster and many species of crab. Squat lobsters and the occasional crayfish can be found in cracks in the walls and when the current runs vast shoals of mackerel, whiting and pollack dart in and out of the gullies. Visibility can be extraordinary with 15m being the norm and 25m commonly experienced. Early in the year the area is saturated in mating nudibranchs and sleepy dogfish whilst in the late spring an abundance of plankton brings in the basking shark. Sunfish arrive in summer, immediately identifiable by their tendency to lie horizontally on the surface of the sea waving their pectoral fins in the air. As summer comes to an end it is not uncommon to spot turtles, dolphins and even various species of whale.

Mating spider crabs

Close-up of spider crab

61

Sixty-one

Kettle's Bottom

Type Reef **Level** Sport diver
Depth 5-14m

Launch Penzance, Sennen
and Lamorna Cove.
Air and dive shop Trevair, Undersea
Adventures and Mount's Bay Diving.

Position 50°04.085'N
005°43.880'W

Description
This rocky outcrop dries at low
water and is situated half-way
between Land's End and the
Longships.

How/when to dive
The reef must be dived on a neap
slack water which is at high
water Newlyn.

What you are likely to see
The area's marine life is similar
to that of the Armed Knight
(Dive 59).

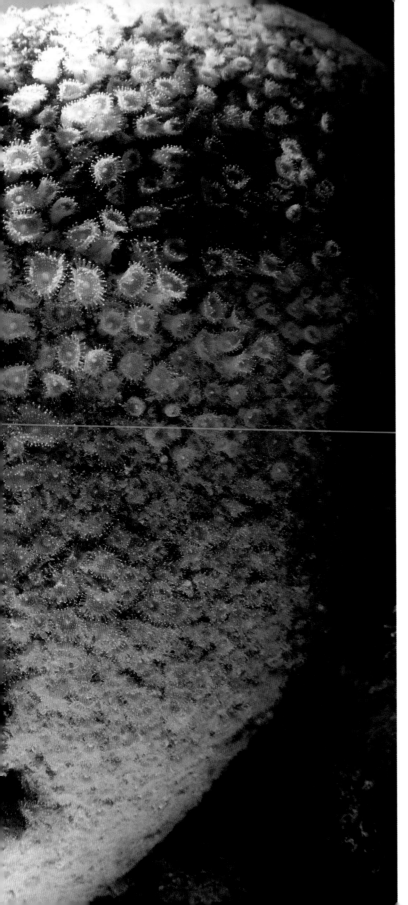

Jewel anemones

62

Sixty-two

Fillis

Type Reef and drift **Level** Sport diver
Depth 7-25m

Launch Penzance, Sennen
and Lamorna Cove.
Air and dive shop Trevair, Undersea
Adventures and Mount's Bay Diving.

Position 50°04.190'N
005°44.220'W

Description
Fillis is an isolated rock that dries at low
water spring tides.

How/when to dive
The reef must be dived at slack water on
a neap, which is at high water Newlyn.
Alternatively, the general area makes
quite an exhilarating drift dive except
on a spring tide where the current is
too strong.

What you are likely to see
The bottom consists of flat rocks with
the occasional boulder, turning to
shingle towards the north. There is
little kelp as it cannot hold due to the
smoothness of the rock and the strong
current. Spider crabs are numerous and
it is also a good place to spot the rare
clingfish that hide in the coarse shingle.
Flounders and other flatties are common
here but they camouflage themselves
superbly against the rock.

4

Around Cape Cornwall and on to St Ives

Above the surface the cliffs are bleak and desolate. Facing towards the north they cannot enjoy the warmth of the summer sun and are often exposed to the full force of winter storms. Dotted along the cliff tops are the many remains of now-silent tin mines, giving a feeling that time has stood still.

This area of coastline is probably one of the least documented dive sites on England's coast. This is probably because the only launch and recovery sites are at its extremities - Sennen to the south and Hayle to the east. What is more, both these slipways have their own problems: the launching at Sennen is very steep and the sand can get quite soft so a four-wheel drive is essential, while Hayle is tidal with a dangerous bar at its entrance. However, don't be put off by this inconvenience, as the diving is just as good as the rest of Cornwall. The best dive in the area – the Wra or Three Stone Oar – is overlooked by Pendeen Watch with its lighthouse and gigantic foghorn. Here, as is common with most of the north coast, the visibility can be outstanding. The tide washes out any silt leaving the sea bed clear of detritus and on a sunny day the sand reflects the sunlight back from the sea bed enhancing the water clarity even further. There are numerous shoals of sand eels which I have spent many an hour observing as whiting and pollack stalk them. The hunters change colour and become almost the same as the sand. On spotting an unsuspecting eel they dart into the shoal at tremendous speed and pick off their victim.

It is important to remember the area's remoteness because it means that few people would spot a flare out at sea, so it is strongly advisable to contact the coastguard at the start of each day to inform them of your intentions - but don't forget to let them know when you return!

Emerald waters inside of the Mozens

63

Sixty-three

Shark's Fin

Type Reef **Level** Sport diver
Depth 5-25m

Launch Lamorna Cove
Penzance and Sennen.
Air and dive shop Trevair, Undersea
Adventures and Mount's Bay Diving.

Position 50°04.515'N
005°44.140'W

Description

So-called because at low water it looks
like a giant shark's dorsal fin, this reef
is just covered at high water and has
claimed a few unaware dive boats.

How/when to dive

The reef must be dived on a neap at
slack water which is at high water
Newlyn. Be very careful approaching
at high water as the rock comes to just
below the surface, but it can usually be
spotted as the water swirls around it.

What you are likely to see

The area is similar to the Armed
Knight (Dive 59) but more spectacular.
Shark's Fin has claimed numerous
commercial wrecks in the past so
wreckage can be found in most of the
surrounding gullies.

Cuckoo wrasse attacks edible sea-urchin

64

Sixty-four

SS Beaumaris

Type Wreck, shore and reef
Level Novice diver **Depth** 8m

Air and dive shop Trevair,
Undersea Adventures and
Mount's Bay Diving.

Position 50°04.740'N
005°41.950'W

Description

This 290ft-long, 2,372 gross ton tanker was an armed cargo ship torpedoed off the Longships on 7 February 1918 by the German U-boat U-53. The Sennen lifeboat assisted in rescuing the majority of the crew while the captain managed to ground her in the shallow waters of Whitesand Bay.

How/when to dive

The wreck can be dived at all states of the tide but the water is very shallow at low water springs. It can be dived from a RIB but as it is 50-200m offshore (depending upon the state of the tide) it is best shore-dived. Walk down the steps in the middle of the beach car park at Sennen. There are two rocky outcrops with a flat bit of sand in the middle. Once at the water's edge swim on a bearing of 330° which should bring you to the wreck site. Be careful if there is an onshore wind, especially at high tide, as the surf can be quite large.

What you are likely to see

She is very broken-up but some of her plates and frames shelter a whole host of juvenile fish, especially wrasse. If you look carefully in the surrounding sand there are usually quite a few flatfish including a rumoured semi-resident turbot. The sand often moves quite dramatically after a ferocious storm and the wreck seems to take on a different appearance on each dive. She also makes a good training site.

Sixty-five

Cowloe Rocks

Type Reef **Level** Sport diver
Depth 12-27m

Launch Sennen
Air and dive shop Trevair, Undersea
Adventures and Mount's Bay Diving.

Position 50°04.820'N
005°42.365'W

Description
A sheer rock face drops from the surface
to a ledge at 12m then carries on to
around 27m.

How/when to dive
The best diving is towards the north-
west tip. This makes a good alternative
dive if the weather is too rough to
venture further out. Avoid the flood
and ebb of a spring tide.

What you are likely to see
Although fairly spectacular the life
is not as prolific as the offshore sites
but the walls do have the usual marine
species of the surrounding area.
Dolphins regularly come into the cove
and this is a good place to spot them.

The steep walls of Cowloe Rocks

Common octopus

Sixty-six

The Brisons

Type Reef **Level** Sport diver
Depth 12-25m

Launch Sennen
Air and dive shop Trevair, Undersea Adventures and Mount's Bay Diving.

Position 50°07.200'N
005°43.220'W

Description

The Brisons is a large rock once home to the northern-most sighting of a sea lion. It is also the venue for the annual swimming race from Cape Cornwall.

How/when to dive

The area can be dived at all states of the tide except the flood and ebb on springs. The better diving is on the seaward side about 25m offshore. The site is also suitable for novices with some open water experience.

What you are likely to see

Above 12m the kelp is quite thick so it is best to head west and dive in slightly deeper water. The site is renowned for numerous wrasse, with many different species sheltering in the gullies and rocky outcrops. Octopus are also quite common although fairly difficult to spot and the anemones and cup corals are larger than most. Bass and mullet can usually be found in the shallow water.

Edible sea-urchin

67 Sixty-seven

The Malta

Type Wreck **Level** Sport diver
Depth 15m

Launch Sennen
Air and dive shop Trevair, Undersea Adventures and Mount's Bay Diving.

Position 50°08.215'N
005°42.701'W

Description

The Malta was a 303ft, 2,244-ton, brig-rigged cargo and passenger ship owned by the Cunard Steamship Company. She ran ashore in fog about half a mile east of Cape Cornwall and sank on 15 October 1889. Most of the cargo of copper, iron, tin plate, herrings, sugar, guano oil, nitrate and palm oil was salvaged. However, many personal baggage and valuables were loaded into the ship's lifeboat which subsequently capsized near Cape Cornwall.

How/when to dive

The wreck is diveable at any time on neaps but slack is required on springs.

What you are likely to see

The wreck is now well broken-up and at times this is more of a reef dive. There are still copper ingots and silver-plated Cunard items that are occasionally found today and cuckoo wrasse frequent the area due to an abundance of sea urchins.

Common lobster

68

Sixty-eight

The Wra or Three Stone Oar

Type Reef **Level** Sport diver
Depth 12-35m

Launch Sennen
Air and dive shop Trevair, Undersea Adventures and Mount's Bay Diving.

Position 50°10.100'N
005°40.040'W

Description

As the name suggests the area consists of three rocks that are dry at all states of the tide. This is another excellent site and very clean like Carn Base. This is probably due to the very strong current that often flows around the rocks. When this happens the wash created can be seen clearly from the cliff tops.

How/when to dive

Slack water is just after high water Newlyn on neaps but you can nearly always find shelter at any state of the tide. A reef runs parallel to the inshore rocks (south-west to north-east) about 30m seaward. It starts at around 12m and quickly descends to 30m or more. Travelling south-east and at right angles to the reef the sea bed turns to sand in about 15m of water.

What you are likely to see

In the summer the sand is crowded with whiting and pollack that hunt the vast shoals of sand eels. It is possible to spend an entire dive just observing and photographing this fascinating spectacle. The visibility is usually superb and only helped by the reflection of sunlight off the sand. The reef is home to numerous huge dahlia anemones – sometimes in clusters of ten or more. Spider crab, edible crab and lobster are also very common and sunfish are often sighted in the summer.

Diver with basking shark

Sixty-nine

Bann Shoal

Type Reef **Level** Advanced diver
Depth 19-50m

Launch Sennen and Hayle.
Air and dive shop Trevair, Undersea
Adventures, Mount's Bay Diving
and Dive St Ives.

Position 50°19.585'N
005°45.801'W

Description

This truly isolated patch of stunning gullies and walls lies just over ten miles north-north-west of Pendeen.

How/when to dive

The area must be dived on slack water which is at high and low water Newlyn. Perfect sea conditions with no ground swell are required.

What you are likely to see

Bann Shoal is one of the most remote dives in this guide. Its location is swept by the main tide so the visibility is usually in excess of 15m. The shallowest part is at about 20m which rapidly drops off to

30-35m. The hard granite-faced rocks are covered in jewel anemones, sponges and hydroids. On the many ledges there are numerous lobster and crab and the occasional crayfish. Towards the bottom of the gullies bright sand reflects the light giving stunning visibility at depth. Here you can find megrim – a flatfish found in abundance in Cornish waters. They normally live below 50m so are rarely seen elsewhere in the British Isles. In early summer on a calm day basking sharks, dolphins and sunfish sometimes congregate around the shoal and I have managed to see all three from the surface at the same time.

Bass hunting sand eels

70

Seventy

The Mozens

Type Reef **Level** Novice diver
Depth 12m

Launch Sennen and Hayle.
Air and dive shop Trevair, Undersea
Adventures, Mount's Bay Diving
and Dive St Ives.

Position 50°10.221'N
          005°39.332'W

Description
This crescent-shaped series of pinnacles rises from a sandy sea bed to within a few metres of the surface.

How/when to dive
On a neap tide the Mozens can be dived at any time but on springs slack water is required, which is one hour either side of high and low water Newquay. If there is any swell the site suffers from underwater surges and should really be avoided.

What you are likely to see
If these pinnacles were in the Red Sea they would have names like 'inner temple', 'near gardens' or 'bass reef'.

This is a fantastic introduction to UK diving for the newcomer, photographer or any diver interested in observing fish behaviour. The pinnacles themselves provide homes for the usual marine invertebrates. The kelp affords shelter to many species of juvenile fish including whiting, pollack and a variety of wrasse. However, the most stunning residents are the prolific sand eels. Hundreds of thousands of them provide a rich feeding ground for bass, sunfish, pollack and whiting. If you settle gently on the sand and let the eels get used to your presence they will eventually surround you. When this happens stay motionless and let the feeding commence.

71

Seventy-one

The Lyminge and Gurnard's Head

Type Reef and wreck
Level Novice diver **Depth** 11m

Launch Sennen and Hayle.
Air and dive shop Trevair, Undersea
Adventures, Mount's Bay Diving
and Dive St Ives.

Position 50°11.705'N
005°36.076'W

Description

The Lyminge was a 261ft, 1,757-ton
steam-driven cargo vessel which struck
Ebal Rock at Gurnard's Head on 19
September 1933. Today it is a fairly
broken wreck but makes an interesting
second dive and is good for novices with
some open water experience.

How/when to dive

The wreck needs to be dived on
slack which is 15 minutes before
high and low water Newquay. Ebal
Rock is the most north-westerly
rock off Gurnard's Head. The main
part of the wreck is on the right of
Ebal Rock while the three triple-
expansion boilers are to the left.

What you are likely to see

The wreckage hosts a myriad of marine
organisms with huge jewel anemones
and plenty of juvenile fish hiding among
the twisted metal. The reef itself is a series
of gullies with plenty of large dahlia
anemones. In the summer you can see
lobster and even crayfish.

Dragonet

72
Seventy-two

The Denebola

Type Wreck **Level** Sport diver
Depth 28m

Launch Hayle
Air and dive shop Trevair, Undersea
Adventures, Mount's Bay Diving
and Dive St Ives.

Position 50°13.234'N
005°37.120'W

Description
The Denebola was struck by two
torpedoes on her starboard side, abreast
of the second and third hatches, on
17 August 1918. She sank almost
immediately with all but two of her
crew managing to take life-rafts and
survive. She was a steel, steam, cargo
vessel of 242ft and 1,481 tons. Four of its
portholes were recovered by a local diver in
a single dive some years ago.

How/when to dive
It needs to be dived on slack water
which is 15 minutes before high and
low water Newquay.

What you are likely to see
The wreck is well broken-up but further
sightings of portholes keep being
reported. Each year after the winter
storms various bits of it are uncovered
or lost due to the shift in the level of
sand. Its superstructure provides shelter
for numerous juvenile fish and small,
friendly, congers can be found among
its plates.

Diver finds a crayfish

Grey seals come for a closer look

73
Seventy-three

Seal Island or
The Carracks

Type Reef **Level** Sport diver
Depth 8-22m

Launch Hayle
Air and dive shop Trevair, Undersea
Adventures, Dive St Ives and
Mount's Bay Diving.

Position 50°12.820'N
005°33.180'W

Description
As the name suggests this island is home to many Atlantic grey seals. Most of them are timid but every now and then a playful one will come and nibble your fins.

How/when to dive
The area can be dived at all states on a neap tide and at slack on springs, which is at high and low water Newquay. Diving can take place all around the rocks although the seaward side is by far the prettiest. Coxswains should take great care as there are several uncharted rocks that lie just below the surface.

What you are likely to see
Seals! Most of the time they prefer to follow you around occasionally nipping your fins. It's a mistake trying to chase them as they simply swim away. The females are the friendliest but keep an eye out for the bulls. There hasn't been a known attack by one on a diver but as they are much bigger than the females they could cause harm simply because of their size. The surrounding area incorporates large gullies that often contain a sleeping seal, otherwise anglerfish, dogfish and numerous blennies are common along with a variety of exquisite anemones.

74
Seventy-four
The Enrico Parodi

Type Wreck **Level** Sport diver
Depth 22m

Launch Hayle
Air and dive shop Trevair, Undersea
Adventures, Dive St Ives and
Mount's Bay Diving.

Position 50°13.040'N
005°33.308'W

Description
This 339ft-long, 3,818-ton, steel-hulled vessel was previously called the Boscombe and before that the King Edgar. She struck Gurnard's Head in thick fog on 21 July 1916. Later, while in tow of the Lady of Isles and bound for St Ives, she sank a few hundred metres off the Carracks.

How/when to dive
The wreck must be dived at slack water which is at high and low water Newquay.

What you are likely to see
It lies broken-up as it was heavily salvaged in the mid-seventies, with its engine-room being the highest part standing some 7m off the sea bed. Shoals of whiting are common as well as breeding cuttlefish, which is evident from the numerous egg clusters on the metal beams.

Cuttlefish

Brill

75

Seventy-five

The Dux

Type Wreck **Level** Sport diver
Depth 33m

Launch Hayle
Air and dive shop Trevair, Undersea Adventures, Dive St Ives and Mount's Bay Diving.

Position 50°15.783-820'N
005°32.419'W

Description

The Dux was a 241ft, 1,349-ton steamship which was torpedoed by the German submarine U-54 during the first World War on 8 May 1918. All her crew survived although her master was taken prisoner, only to be released the next day.

How/when to dive

It must be dived at slack water which is at high and low water Newquay.

What you are likely to see

The Dux lies broken up and scattered over a shingle sea bed. Its three boilers stand about 4m proud of the sea bed but its keel and hull are usually covered in sand. On a sunny day light reflects off it giving amazing visibility. Quite a few shoals of bib and whiting seek shelter among its ribs in the otherwise featureless seascape. John Dory are also quite common in late summer.

Close-up of a plaice

76

Seventy-six

SS Kintuck

Type Wreck **Level** Sport diver
Depth 33m

Launch Hayle
Air and dive shop Trevair, Undersea
Adventures, Mount's Bay Diving
and Dive St Ives.

Position 50°14.439'N
005°32.011'W and
50°14.390'N
005°31.890'W

Description

SS Kintuck was a 412ft, 4,639-ton schooner-rigged Blue Funnel steamer which sank on 2 December 1917 after being torpedoed by UC-17. All except one seaman survived. The wreck lists slightly to port with its bows pointing east towards St Ives.

How/when to dive

The wreck must be dived on slack water which is at high and low water Hayle (one hour before high and low water Milford Haven).

What you are likely to see

The Kintuck is quite broken-up except for the boilers and engine-room. The bow stands upright and looks like a steeple when viewed from a distance. To the south-west there is a vast array of condenser tubes sprawled over the sea bed. The stern section lies some way off at the second position given. Towards the stern the prop shaft is clearly visible, but the prop was salvaged in the early 1970s. She lies on a sandy bottom which reflects the sunlight to give an eerie scene – almost as if the wreck were lit from beneath.

Seventy-seven

The St Chamond or Train wreck

Type Wreck **Level** Sport diver
Depth 26m

Launch Hayle
Air and dive shop Trevair, Undersea Adventures, Dive St Ives and Mount's Bay Diving.

Position 50°14.861'N
005°29.833'W

Whiting

Description

The 314ft, 3,077-ton St Chamond was sunk without any loss of life by U-60 on April 30th 1918. Among her documented cargo were five 75-ton steam-engines, hence its nickname the Train Wreck, however some local divers claim that there are actually seven.

How/when to dive

The wreck must be dived on slack water which is at high and low water Hayle (one hour before high and low water Milford Haven).

What you are likely to see

The wreck is fairly broken-up but the main attraction is the relatively intact locomotives. They are easy to find with three lying on the starboard side and two on the port side. There are also numerous pipes scattered about the wreck which provide homes for conger eels and juvenile invertebrates. One of the boilers stands proud of the sea bed on the port side while the second has mysteriously disappeared. The steel propeller and rudder lie almost at right angles to the rest of the wreck on the starboard side. Quite a few bib and whiting shoal around and visibility is generally in excess of 10m.

78

Seventy-eight

The Zone

Type Wreck **Level** Sport diver
Depth 32m

Launch Hayle
Air and dive shop Trevair, Undersea
Adventures, Dive St Ives and
Mount's Bay Diving.

Position 50°16.372-429'N
005°29.287-359'W

Description

The Zone was a large steamship
some 360ft in length, weighing 3,914
tons. She was torpedoed by the
German submarine U-110 and sunk
on 30 December 1917. Today it is still
fairly intact.

How/when to dive

It must be dived on slack water
which is at high and low water Hayle
(one hour before high and low water
Milford Haven).

What you are likely to see

There are two large boilers with resident
congers in quite a few of their holes. Five
metres to the north and running down
the majority of the wreck is the propeller
shaft, about a metre off the sea bed and
still on its stands. As it was an armed
vessel, shell cases are occasionally found
towards its stern. This is a very scenic
wreck which is often surrounded by a
large shoal of bib and when visibility is
good you can get a clear, well-lit view of
the whole of the wreck.

Bib

Jewel anemone

79
Seventy-nine
Porthminster Reef

Type Reef **Level** Novice diver
Depth 7-18m

Launch Hayle
Air and dive shop Trevair, Undersea
Adventures, Mount's Bay Diving
and Dive St Ives.

Position 50°12.500'N
005°28.100'W

Description
This shallow site is just a two-minute
boat ride from the harbour at St Ives.

How/when to dive
The reef can be dived at all states of
the tide.

What you are likely to see
This is a great shallow dive for
photographers, novices or for just
observing the diversity of marine life.
Throughout the summer triggerfish,
sunfish and John Dory are common, as
well as lobster, edible crab and spider
crab. On rare occasions, in shallow,
weedy waters, seahorses can be found.

Short-snouted
sea-horse

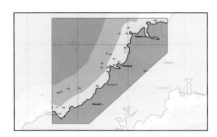

5

Spectacular and rugged, the North Coast

It is difficult to imagine that anywhere in Cornwall could be more rugged than the cliffs of Land's End, but the north coast is the most exposed of all Cornwall's coastline. It is hammered by unforgiving north winds and coupled with the fact that there are few places to launch a boat, it is not dived as extensively as the south coast. This is a shame because the visibility is nearly always good due to the lack of any major river system flowing into the area. Visibility is further enhanced by the lack of silt on the sea bed which is either rock or coarse sand. There is the wreck of the Pandora with her resident swarm of conger eels. There is the fairly intact remains of the Sphene which, when conditions are perfect, can be observed in its entirety from just below the surface. Finally there are the many spectacular reefs such as Divers' Rock that are swept by strong tides providing nutrient-rich waters for a whole host of invertebrate life and crustaceans.

The coastline itself consists mainly of tall cliffs interspersed with popular and picturesque holiday towns such as St Ives, Newquay and Padstow. Tourism has replaced the once slow-paced life of the fishing villages, providing an abundance of places to eat and to stay. A perfect destination for divers with children.

Smugglers' Cave

Short-spined sea scorpion

80

Eighty

Fanny Lambert

Type Wreck **Level** Advanced diver
Depth 44m

Launch Hayle
Air and dive shop Trevair, Undersea
Adventures, Dive St Ives and
Mount's Bay Diving.

Position 50°19.560'N
005°28.590'W

Description
She was a 201ft-long, 699-ton, three-masted, steam cargo vessel which sank during a horrific storm on 6 February 1867 with total loss of life.

How/when to dive
The wreck must be dived on slack which is 30 minutes after high and low water Newquay.

What you are likely to see
It is fairly broken-up with two curiously square boilers. Underneath these lie the clearly visible remains of the brass helm which is jammed against the sea bed. Bib, pollack and whiting are common shoaling around what remains of its superstructure. She is also home to a suprising number of short-spined scorpion-fish.

Plumose anemones cover the wreck

81

Eighty-one

The Pandora

Type Wreck **Level** Advanced diver
Depth 42m

Launch Hayle
Air and dive shop Trevair, Undersea
Adventures, Dive St Ives and
Mount's Bay Diving.

Position 50°19.857-71'N
005°28.572'W

Description
The identification of this wreck is uncertain, but it appears to have been a large steamer with a cargo of Nissen Huts.

How/when to dive
Must be dived on slack which is 30 minutes after high and low water Newquay.

What you are likely to see
Of all the wrecks in sport diving range out of St Ives Bay this is the most intact. The highest point is at 35m on the stern. The bow, midships and engine-room are clearly visible with only the side of the wreck damaged. Quite a few shoals of large pollack, whiting and bib are always present. Inside the wreck there are huge conger eels and rust-coloured lobster. Just off the wreck, 10m to the west, lies a clump of Ross coral more than a metre in diameter.

Diver inspects a capstan

Eighty-two

The Lifting Vessel

Type Wreck **Level** Sport diver
Depth 24m

Launch Hayle
Air and dive shop Trevair, Undersea
Adventures, Dive St Ives and
Mount's Bay Diving.

Position 50°14.370- 385'N
005°26.259'W

Description

This was an engineless barge that held the cable of a barrage balloon during World War II. For years it has been rumoured that there are two sets of old brass diving helmets on board but none has ever been recovered.

How/when to dive

This should be dived at slack water which is at high and low water Newquay.

What you are likely to see

There is a massive bow standing some 6m off the sea bed complete with huge rollers for the anchor chain. It is relatively intact with no main engine or propeller present – obviously – but there is an engine to operate the crane which has now collapsed. Visibility is generally quite good and this makes a good second dive.

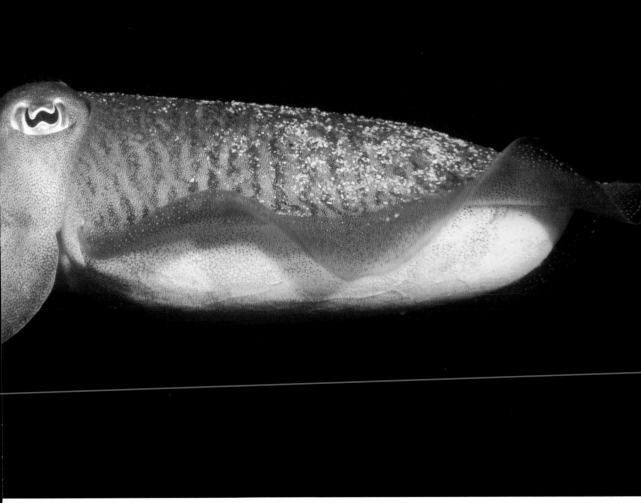

Cuttlefish

Eighty-three

The Gleno

Type Wreck **Level** Advanced diver
Depth 45m

Launch Hayle
Air and dive shop Trevair, Undersea
Adventures, Dive St Ives and
Mount's Bay Diving.

Position 50°20.366'N
005°25.770-850'W

Description

This small cargo vessel, 112ft-long and weighing 187 tons, was hit by a storm while trying to make for shelter in the lee of Lundy Island. When her cargo of flour shifted she capsized and sank on 31 January 1917.

How/when to dive

The Glenco must be dived on slack water which is 30 minutes after high and low water Newquay.

What you are likely to see

The bow and stern are relatively intact although the propeller is missing. The midships are starting to collapse and the mast has fallen. It makes for quite a deep and sometimes dark dive but has plenty of marine life, including some large cuttlefish which can be found in the summer.

Jewel anemones

84
Eighty-four

The Princess Royal

Type Wreck **Level** Advanced diver
Depth 39m

Launch Hayle
Air and dive shop Trevair, Undersea
Adventures, Dive St Ives and
Mount's Bay Diving.

Position 50°19.394'N
005°19.954'W

Description

This 294ft, 1,986-ton Scottish cargo
vessel was hit under her port bow by
a torpedo from the German submarine
U-101 on 26 May 1918. All of her seven
crew where picked up by patrol vessels
and landed at St Ives.

How/when to dive

Although fairly broken-up, it is easy
to find on the echo-sounder. It must
be dived on slack water, which is 20
minutes after high and low water
Newquay.

What you are likely to see

The wreck is spread out over a large
area. In places it stands 8m proud of the
sea bed, rising to 10m at the bow and
stern. Portholes are still found, although
I particularly enjoy this wreck for the
vast amount of fish life. Because it lies
quite a way offshore on a featureless
sea bed, she acts as a haven for juvenile
fish. This in turn attracts some huge
pollack and cod as well as whiting. The
flattened superstructure also provides
homes for conger eel and lobster.

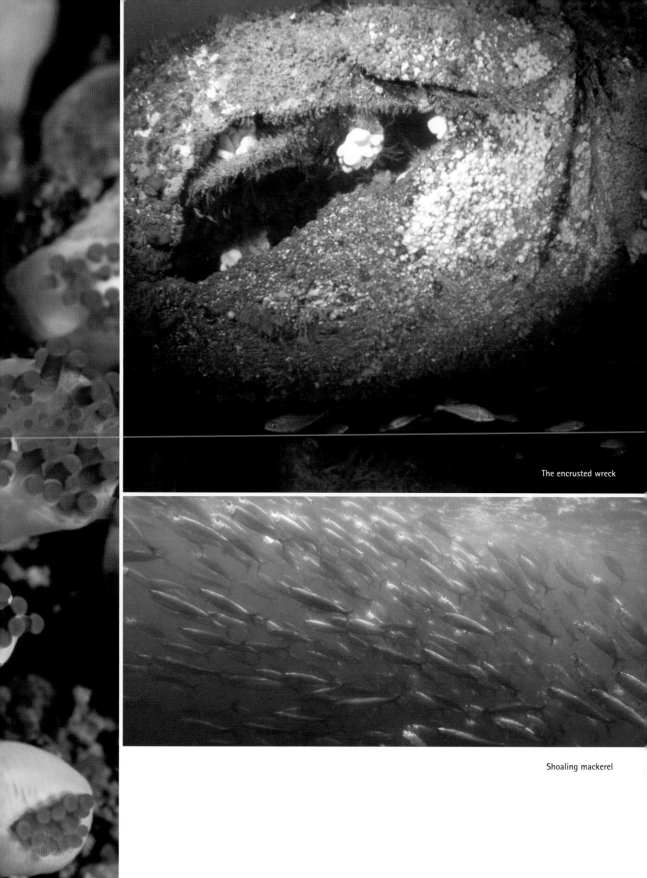

The encrusted wreck

Shoaling mackerel

Crayfish

85
Eighty-five
Bawden Rocks

Type Reef and drift
Level Sport diver **Depth** 10-40m

Launch Newquay
Air and dive shop Koolair
and Dive Newquay.

Position 50°20.000'N
005°13.860'W

Description
Lying just under a mile offshore and exposed to the full force of the tide Bawden Rocks is a fantastic scenic dive. During the Second World War they were used for target practice by the RAF. Consequently there are lots of bullets from the guns of Spitfires and Mosquitoes surrounding the area.

How/when to dive
Slack water is about one hour after high and low water Hayle. On a neap tide you can drift dive them off slack.

What you are likely to see
Inside the rocks the depth is between 10-12m. Venturing seaward brings you to a wall that drops to 40m. There is a huge amount of dead man's fingers and plumose anemones, while the gullies and cracks in the rocks often have large crab and lobster – even crayfish in the summer. Shoals of mackerel, mullet and bass are not uncommon. If you look carefully on the sea bed you may even find some bullets.

86

Eighty-six

Carter's Rocks

Type Reef and drift **Level** Sport diver
Depth 0-22m

Launch Newquay
Air and dive shop Koolair
and Dive Newquay.

Position 50°23.480'N
005°09.550'W

Description
Locally known as 'Mad Rips' due to the strong current that flows off slack water, Carter's Rocks support a profusion of marine life. They are dry at all states of the tide, so they are easy to find.

How/when to dive
Slack water is about one hour after high and low water Hayle and you can drift dive them on a neap tide.

What you are likely to see
Inshore there is much evidence of ship wreckage but strangely there are few reports of any ship foundering there. To the west the rocks are covered in a huge variety of anemones which attract large shoals of fish. This is an excellent scenic dive and great for photography on slack water.

Jewel anemones

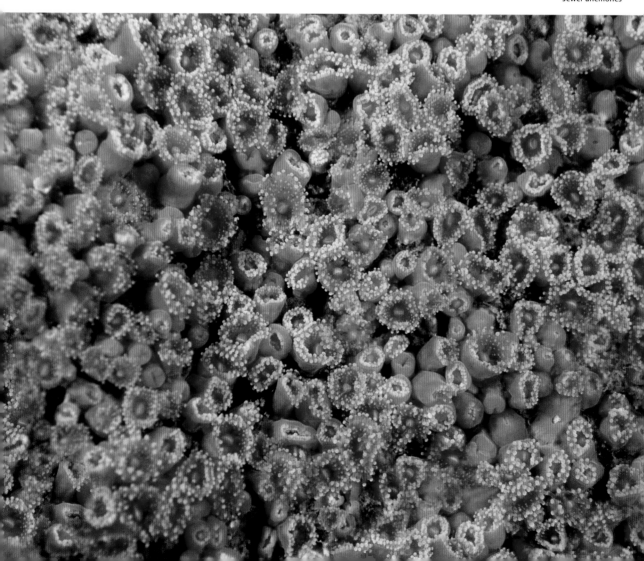

Conger eel hunts for hiding prey

Eighty-seven

The Orford Ness

Type Wreck **Level** Sport diver
Depth 34m

Launch Newquay
Air and dive shop Koolair
and Dive Newquay.

Position 50°24.650-744'N
005°11.150-233'W

Description
The Orford Ness was a 2,790-ton, 332ft steamship that was torpedoed by U-60 on 20 August 1918. It lies on her port side with its stern broken away. The two boilers stand some 5m high while the steel screw is half-buried to the south-west of the main wreck.

How/when to dive
Dive at slack water which is 15 minutes after high and low water Newquay.

What you are likely to see
The wreck is in two sections and fairly broken-up. The two prominent parts are around the bow and its two boilers but there is also a profusion of winches. There are friendly congers eels that frequently swim out of hiding to greet the visiting diver. Bib, whiting and pollack are also common.

Stinging hydroids

88

Eighty-eight

The Chick

Type Reef and drift **Level** Sport diver
Depth 10-17m

Launch Newquay
Air and dive shop Koolair
and Dive Newquay.

Position 50°24.320'N
005°08.920'W

Description
This dive is similar to Carter's Rocks but in shallower water. The best diving is to the south-west of the rock.

How/when to dive
Slack water is about one hour after high and low water Hayle and you can drift dive them on a neap tide.

What you are likely to see
The reef is a continuation of the headland and the best diving is on the seaward side where there are plenty of gullies to explore. All kinds of macro life clings to the rocks and numerous tiny crustaceans are common in the summer months. This also makes quite a good site for novices with some open water experience and for drift-dive training.

Red fingers

Bib

Kelp

89

Eighty-nine

West Pentier

Type Reef and drift **Level** Novice diver
Depth 10m

Launch Newquay
Air and dive shop Koolair
and Dive Newquay.

Position 50°24.520'N
005°8.150'W

Description
The reef consists of a series of gullies
running perpendicular to the shore. It
makes a superb site for the second or
third dive of the day and is ideal for
training and photography.

How/when to dive
You can dive at any state of the tide
and the best area is just beneath the
Lewinnick Lodge bar and restaurant,
which can be seen on the cliff top.

What you are likely to see
It can be quite thick with kelp by mid-
summer, but this does provide a perfect
habitat for a whole host of juvenile
species of marine life. The best way to
dive the site is to try to dive underneath
the kelp. This requires good buoyancy
skills and also means you have to move
very slowly. The reward, however, is that
you observe all the macro life which
otherwise often gets overlooked – one
such critter is the fabulously coloured
Norwegian topknot which can be
perfectly camouflaged against the
surrounding rocks.

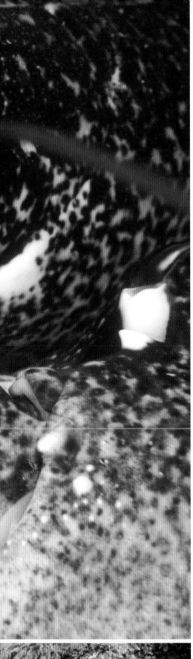

90 Ninety

The Goose

Type Reef and drift **Level** Sport diver
Depth 10-18m

Launch Newquay
Air and dive shop Koolair
and Dive Newquay.

**Position 50°24.740'N
005°07.700'W**

Description
The Goose can often have a strong current flowing off slack water. This means that similarly to Carter's Rock it supports a great deal of marine life. Likewise the Goose is dry at all states of the tide and therefore easy to find.

How/when to dive
Slack water is about one hour after high and low water Hayle and you can drift dive on a neap tide.

What you are likely to see
The north-west tip is the where the marine life is best. A series of gullies drop away to a rock and shingle sea bed at about 18m. The visibility is generally excellent and if diving in a current you will find huge shoals of mackerel, bass and scad or horse mackerel, which frequent the shallow waters just off the point.

91 Ninety-one

Madusa Rock

Type Reef and drift
Level Advanced diver **Depth** 25-35m

Launch Newquay
Air and dive shop Koolair
and Dive Newquay.

**Position 50°25.600-26.200'N
005°10.600-11.200'W**

Description
Madusa Rock is a spectacular offshore reef system about five miles west of Newquay. There is some wreckage of a steam trawler at 50°25.730'N 005°11.083'W.

How/when to dive
Slack water is 15 minutes after high and low water Newquay. Alternatively it makes an excellent drift dive off slack, but avoid high spring tides as the current is too strong.

What you are likely to see
The whole area is covered in a thick carpet of dead man's fingers giving a 'furry' feel to the site. The sea bed is fairly flat but rocky outcrops provide the perfect shelter for crab, lobster and crayfish. Among the dead man's fingers are a whole host of other soft corals and sponges, with huge anglerfish, sole and flounder also common. Visibility is usually excellent with 15m the norm. It is a pity that the relatively deep depth results in such a short dive.

Common lobster

Sea beard

92

Ninety-two

The Shell Wreck

Type Wreck **Level** Advanced diver
Depth 38-42m

Launch Newquay
Air and dive shop Koolair
and Dive Newquay.

Position 50°27.733'N
005°09.025'W

Description
The exact identity of this wreck remains a mystery although it is believed to have been an armed merchant vessel which was either mined or torpedoed during World War II.

How/when to dive
Slack water is one hour after high and low water Newquay.

What you are likely to see
As the name suggests the wreck has many anti-aircraft shells which can be found towards the stern lying beside the propeller – it is advisable to leave these well alone! The wreck itself is fairly broken-up but the bow and stern can be clearly made out. Despite its relatively deep depth it is usually quite bright and on a sunny day the entire wreck can be seen.

93

Ninety-three

The Lake Edon

Type Wreck **Level** Advanced diver
Depth 35m

Launch Newquay.
Air and dive shop Koolair
and Dive Newquay.

Position 50°27.604-615'N
005°07.586-597'W

Description

The Lake Edon was a 2,371-ton American cargo steamship which was lost on 21 August 1918 after being torpedoed by the German submarine U-107. Often referred to as the 'middle wreck' she lies between the wrecks of the Siracusa and the Shell.

How/when to dive

Slack water is one hour after high and low water Newquay.

What you are likely to see

The wreck lies fairly broken-up as it was heavily salvaged some years ago, but in the same way as other wrecks in the area it provides a safe artificial reef for fish – bib, pollack and conger eel are common. The boilers that drove its three-cylinder, triple-expansion engine sit proud of the sea bed by about 6m and are covered with hydroids and anemones. Towards the stern its davits also stand out to a height of 3m, near the scattered remains of a cast-iron propeller.

94
Ninety-four

The Siracusa

Type Wreck **Level** Advanced diver
Depth 35m

Launch Newquay
Air and dive shop Koolair
and Dive Newquay.

Position 50°26.417'N
005°06.681'W

Description

The Siracusa was a 1,243-ton schooner-rigged steamship which sank in a fierce gale on 6 March 1897 and now lies just 300m from Newquay Harbour.

How/when to dive

Most dives on the Siracusa start off either at the bow or the boilers. The wreck lies at 35m, with the top of the bow at 27m and the top of the boilers at 25m. It can be dived at all states of the tide on neaps, but must be dived on a slack at spring tides. Slack is one hour after high and low water Newquay.

What you are likely to see

Much of the wreck stands proud of the bottom and, although many divers enjoy finning straight to the propeller, my favourite part of this wreck is the bow, which rises vertically from the sea bed, offering some interesting swim-throughs in the places where it has been broken. You can sit on a bollard situated just beyond the bow on the bottom, and look up at shafts of green light streaming through the holes in the front of the wreck. This is also the place where you are most likely to run into schools of fish – pollack and

Above: Mating velvet
swimming crabs
Right: Red fingers

bib are common. There are two large boilers with a triple expansion steam engine which lies on its side just aft of them. The propeller shafting runs all the way to th stern still supported on its bearings. In late spring the Siracusa becomes home for many breeding crabs. It is possible to swim along the entire length of the Siracusa in one dive, although you will be a bit hurried if you want to avoid a decompression penalty. Much of the superstructure has been stripped by salvors who used explosives to break up the wreck. Visibility is usually in excess of 10m and the cargo of coal is still quite evident.

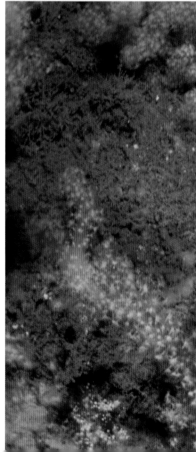

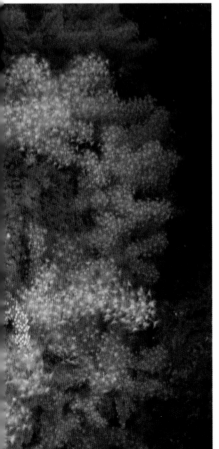

Spider crab and
spikey starfish

95
Ninety-five

Porth Rock

Type Reef **Level** Sport diver
Depth 11-15m

Launch Newquay
Air and dive shop Koolair
and Dive Newquay.

Position 50°25.740'N
005°03.800'W

Description

Just off Trevelgue Head lies a hidden
rock ideal for photography and shallow
diving. It also is a good site for novices
with some open water experience.

How/when to dive

To locate the rock first find the cave on
the seaward side of the island. Line this
up with the last beach hut on Tolcarne
Beach on a bearing of about 170°
magnetic. Run in on this bearing until
you find the rock on the echo-sounder.
It can be dived on all states of the tide.

What you are likely to see

The area surrounding the rock consists
of beautiful gullies and tunnels. There is
a huge variety of marine life including
Ross coral, fan corals, dead man's
fingers, crab and lobster. It is best
known for the profusion of spider crabs
that congregate in their hundreds to
breed in the summer months. Atlantic
triggerfish are also frequent visitors in
late summer.

Jewel anemones

96 Ninety-six

Park Cow or Cow and Calf

Type Reef **Level** Sport diver
Depth 22m

Launch Newquay, Padstow and Rock.
Air and dive shop Koolair
and Dive Newquay.

Position 50°29.720'N
005°02.930'W

Description
This rock lies about 400m offshore from Park Head and is covered at high water. It is quite exposed and prone to swell and fierce currents but it plays host to a spectacular diversity of critters.

How/when to dive
It should only be dived at slack which is one hour after high and low water Newquay. It also needs to be fairly calm with no ground swell present.

What you are likely to see
The seaward side of the rock is a sheer wall that drops to about 22m. Visibility is usually excellent which enables the shoals of mackerel and bass to be seen clearly. All kinds of anemones cling to the rocks and could be described as 'oversized' by comparison with their inshore neighbours. There is plenty of evidence of wreckage but this is probably the remains of numerous ships that have foundered here.

Common shrimp

97

Ninety-seven

Divers' Rock

Type Reef and drift
Level Advanced diver **Depth** 27-40m

Launch Newquay, Padstow and Rock.
Air and dive shop Koolair
and Dive Newquay.

Position 50°32.441'N
005°06.149'W

Description
Of all the reefs in this area Divers' Rock is probably the most spectacular.

How/when to dive
Lying nearly three nautical miles offshore it is very exposed and should only be dived in the calmest of conditions. Slack water is required, which is one hour after high and low water Newquay.

What you are likely to see
Dead man's fingers cover the sea bed as well as numerous species of starfish and brittle stars. There is plenty of wreckage around which has led to the recovery of portholes and ammunition in the past. Among the rocks and plates are quite a few lobsters and crabs, while in deeper waters there are superb red fingers and huge clumps of rose and fan corals.

Dahlia anemones

Ninety-eight

The Quies and the Runswick

Type Wreck and reef **Level** Sport diver
Depth 15-20m

Launch Newquay, Padstow and Rock.
Air and dive shop Koolair
and Dive Newquay.

Position 50°32.717'N
005° 03. 299'W

Description
The Runswick was a 343ft, 3,060-ton steam cargo vessel which sank after being torpedoed by UB-109 on 18 April 1918. She now lies very broken-up on the north-east side of the Quies.

How/when to dive
Slack water is one hour after high and low water Newquay. The boilers and most of the wreckage lie between the inshore island of the Quies and another small rock towards the shore.

What you are likely to see
The area is more of a reef dive than a wreck dive but the Runswick's two boilers are quite evident – one stands on its end some 5m proud of the sea bed. Marine life is better than average with many species of wrasse nesting in the gullies throughout the spring. There are huge dahlia anemones on some of the many plates, as well as enormous shrimps which seem to congregate in the crevices. This site is surprisingly sheltered from a south-west wind if you tuck in behind the islands.

Dahlia anemone

Beadlet anemone

Diver spots a common lobster
in the torch beam

Conger eels make a
home in the wreck

One hundred

The Sphene

Type Wreck **Level** Sport diver
Depth 26m

Launch Padstow and Rock.
Air and dive shop Dive Newquay
and Koolair.

Position 50°36.161'N
004°53.165'W

Description
The Sphene was a 615-ton Glaswegian
collier which sank on 6 February 1946
after hitting Mouls Island in heavy seas.
All the crew were saved before she
drifted eastwards and sank to 25m.

How/when to dive
Slack water is required, which is half an
hour after high and low water Padstow.

What you are likely to see
The wreck is relatively intact, especially
the stern and engine-room. Holes are
starting to appear in her plates and you
can swim through between the rudder
and propeller. The boilers are covered in
marine life as is much of her external
hull. Local clubs have nicknamed her
double hull 'conger alley' due to the
numerous congers that have taken
up residence. Unfortunately the bow
was recently pulled over by a trawling
fishing vessel that caught her net on it.
Watch out for monofilament net.

Ninety-nine

The Saphir

Type Wreck **Level** Sport diver
Depth 33m

Launch Newquay, Padstow and Rock.
Air and dive shop Dive Newquay
and Koolair.

Position 50°33.840'N
005°03.924'W

Description
The Saphir was a 284ft, 1,406-ton
Norwegian steamship which was
torpedoed by the German submarine
U-94 on 25 May 1918.

How/when to dive
Slack water is one hour after high and
low water Newquay.

What you are likely to see
The wreck is quite intact and extremely
picturesque. It lies on its starboard side
but the stern has fallen apart. The hold
can be easily penetrated and provides
shelter for massive pollack, whiting and
shoals of bib. On one occasion we found
a huge lobster roaming around on the
sea bed next to the remains of her hull.

Launch and Recover sites

Fort Bovisand Diving, Plymouth
01752 408021

To get there take the A379 from Plymouth east towards Plymstock, then follow signs to Bovisand beach via Staddon Fort and continue along the single tarmac road to Bovisand dive centre. The slip is accessible at all states of the tide except on low water springs. Parking is limited and fills up early in the day. Fort Bovisand is a dive centre and offers showers, toilets and accommodation. Keep a very good lookout for surface marker buoys belonging to shore divers.

Mount Batten Slip, Plymouth
01752 404567

To get there take the A379 from Plymouth to Kingsbridge. At the first roundabout turn right to Plymstock and follow the road to Hoe and Mount Batten. The Mount Batten Centre is a non-profit charity which encourages affordable watersports for all. The slip is free of charge and is usable at all states of the tide except low water springs. There is a chandlery, bar and restaurant, petrol, parking, toilets, showers and changing rooms all close to hand. There is an 8 knot speed limit in the harbour.

Queen Anne's Battery Marina, Plymouth
01752 671142

To get there take the A38 towards Plymouth and follow the signs to Queen Anne's Battery Marina. This excellent slip is usable at all states of the tide and launching costs £12 which includes car parking. There are restaurants, cafés, bars, shops, petrol, toilets and showers all close by.

Looe Harbour - Mill Pool Car Park
01503 262839

It is situated near the Discovery Centre. Harbour dues are £3.50. The upper ramp area is concrete which turns to mud at the bottom. It is suitable for launching a large RIB two to three hours either side of high tide. Cars and trailers can be left in the pay and display car park. The harbour-master office is on East Looe Quay, above a road bridge. There is also a slipway at Millpool Boatyard close by.

Penmarlam Quay, Bodinnick
01726 832471/2

The slip is found by going through Yeate Farm and caravan site. It costs £5 per day which includes parking (from October to April these need to be five £1 coins). There are showers and toilets and camping for caravans and tents next to the slip. You can launch at any time except at low water springs.

Fowey Harbour - Caffa Mill
01726 832471

To find the slip follow signs from Four Turnings service station to Fowey jetties and Bodinnick car ferries. Caffa Mill car park and slip are next to and just past the ferry queue. Try to avoid Fowey town centre as the streets are very narrow. Harbour dues are £2. The car park is quite a walk so it is best to park your car and walk down to the ferry pick-up point. The RIB can pick you up from there. You can launch at all states of tide. Fowey harbour has a 6 knot speed limit.

Charlestown - Square Sail
01726 67526 / 70241

Charlestown Harbour has moorings afloat in both the inner and outer harbours. There is parking on the quayside for small craft with use of either the slipway or beach for launching and recovery.

Pentewan Sands Holiday Camp
01726 843485

Situated just across the road from Ocean Sports just north of Mevagissey is a large holiday and camping resort. For residents only during June, July and August there is a tractor launch and recovery service at about £10 per day. Outside of these months residents can launch by themselves, however a good four-wheel drive vehicle is required.

Portmellon - Tidal Beach

Launching from this public slipway is only available one hour either side of high water and would be suitable for inflatables or small RIBs only.

Gorran Haven

Launching on this public slipway is from a concrete slip that turns to sand two hours either side of high water. A 4x4 vehicle is then required which enables you to launch at all states of the tide except low water springs. In the peak summer months launching and recovery need to take place either before 10am or after 5pm. There is car parking close by.

Portholland (west)

There is a free public slip that is used by local diving clubs. Launching is at all states of the tide from a concrete slipway then hard sandy beach. There is limited parking on the road but plenty at East Portholland. The road is quite narrow approaching the slipway.

Pendower Beach

This is a public slipway not far from the A3078, suitable for launching and recovery at all states of the tide except low water. A 4x4 vehicle is recommended and there is a reasonable amount of parking on the roadside.

St Mawes

01326 270553

The slipway is behind the harbour wall in the town centre of St Mawes. It is quite a steep concrete slip which allows launching three hours either side of high water. The cost depends on vessel length and is between £4-9. Trailers can be parked at a yard 200m away but car parking can be difficult.

Pasco's Boatyard, St Just-in-Roseland   01326 270269

To get there take the A3078 from Truro towards St Mawes. Turn right onto a narrow road signposted St Just Church and Bar. The slipway is about 1.5km at St Just Creek, Pasco's Boatyard. There is plenty of parking for cars and trailers although it gets very busy on public holidays. It costs £4.10 per day to launch. The ramp is short and ends up on the beach. At low water it can get quite muddy. There is a 5 knot speed restriction in the creek.

Mylor

01326 372121

To get there take the A39 from Truro towards Falmouth. 2km past Devoran, turn left signposted to Mylor Bridge. Go through Mylor Bridge and follow brown signs to Mylor Yacht Harbour. The slipway is opposite the harbour office. It is free to launch and there is quite a large car park adjacent to the slipway. Mylor has an excellent chandlery and there are public toilets. The harbour-master welcomes all divers and is always helpful with local knowledge and advice. There is also a café and the Ganges Restaurant which is very popular. There are two slipways which can be used at all states of the tide except low water springs. There is a 5 knot speed limit in Mylor Creek.

Falmouth Watersports Slip, Falmouth   01326 312285

To get there take the A39 to Falmouth. Entering Falmouth there is a roundabout with McDonald's directly in front of you. Turn left at this roundabout and Falmouth Marina can be found 200m on your left. It costs £10 to launch which includes car and trailer parking. There is a chandlery, restaurant, toilets, showers and shops close by. The slip can be used three and a half hours either side of high water from 8am to 6pm. Be careful when entering or leaving the marina around low tide as there is a ridge which is marked with a depth gauge. There is an 8 knot speed limit in the inner harbour.

Grove Place Boatyard, Falmouth   01326 312285

The slip is at the southern end of Arwenack Street near where it turns into Bar Street and close to the new National Maritime Museum. It costs £5.50 to launch and there is pay and display parking next door but it has a three hour limit. Longer term parking is about ten minutes walk away. There are toilets and an excellent fish and chip shop around the corner. The slip can be used at all states of tide except low water springs. There is an 8 knot speed limit in the inner harbour.

Helford Passage, Mawnan Smith   01326 250770

To get there take the B3291 south from Falmouth and take a left turn to Mawnan Smith. Helford Passage is about another 2km towards the river. No cars are allowed on the beach so launching is done by a local driver with a Land Rover. The launch charge is £10 and can be done on all states of the tide except low water springs. There is a pub next to the slip.

Porthkerris Beach

Porthkerris can be reached by first heading towards St. Keverne. When you get into St. Keverne, follow the road around past the White Hart Pub and then past the fire station towards Porthallow. At the Y junction turn right and first left then follow the road up to the Conservatory Restaurant to check-in. There is an excellent dive centre based there called Porthkerris Divers (see under air and dive shops for facilities). For £10 they will launch and recover your RIB with their tractor. This can be done at all states of the tide and is the perfect base from which to dive the Manacles. There are also overnight moorings and camping is permitted on the beach.

Porthoustock Beach

To get there head towards St Keverne. Follow the road out of St Keverne down into Porthoustock which is signposted. There is no charge but a donation to the beach maintenance fund via the donation box should be made on leaving. It can be used at all states of the tide. A big wide ramp is regularly flattened by JCB but a 4x4 vehicle is recommended. Better still, for £5 per day Dive Action Services will launch and recover your RIB with their tractor. There are toilets at the top of the beach. Keep a look-out for shore divers when using the harbour.

Launching a RIB at Sennen

Porthleven Harbour-master

**01326 574270 (office)
or 563472 (home)**

Found at the end of the B3304 on the east side of Mount's Bay, Porthleven has a good concrete slipway which can be used three hours either side of high water. Fees are £10 per day or £30 per week which includes parking for one car and trailer. Local shops, pubs and restaurants are all close by. It can get very busy in the summer.

Marazion Beach, Penzance

The slip down to the beach is adjacent to the car park behind North Street and is free of charge. The sand is quite hard and slopes gently down to the water's edge - a four-wheel drive is recommended. It can be used at all states of the tide, however on lows it is quite a long way to the water's edge.

Penzance Harbour

01736 366113

Penzance public slipway can be found by turning left into the harbour car park, just after Penzance station, and then keeping to the left towards Albert Pier. Launching is possible up to three and a half hours either side of high water. Cars and trailers are parked in the public car park (pay and display) and harbour dues (£5.50) are paid to the harbour-master. There is a freshwater tap and hose at the top of the slip available to wash your boat and trailer afterwards. There is a 5 knot speed limit in the harbour.

Lamorna Cove

Lamorna Cove has a good slipway, ample parking and a café serving excellent home-made pasties and cakes, as well as a small shop and public toilets. (Note: the car park does fill up quickly on public holidays, especially if the weather is nice, so aim to get there before 9.30am). You will be charged £5 to park your car, and £12 to park your trailer and launch from the slipway. The slipway is right in front of the car park and trailers are left at the far end of the harbour wall. Launching and recovery is generally very easy, unless the wind is southeasterly or the surf is over 1m high. In these situations try to avoid high-tide recovery, as the waves tend to travel along the harbour wall getting amplified as they go - and they peak just where your trailer is. At spring tides and low water the harbour dries out completely, so a good 4x4 drive vehicle is necessary. Lamorna is 6.5km south-west of Penzance at the end of a steep tree-lined road off the B3315.

Sennen

At Sennen, the slipway can be found at the end of Sennen Cove past the lifeboat station and costs £10 to launch. The slipway is extremely steep so it is essential to have a 4x4 drive vehicle and lots of rope! Launching and recovery can be done at all states of tide, except two hours before or after low water on a spring tide. Take careful note of the local regulations, and always give way to fishing vessels, especially when they are launching and recovering. Sennen slipway has been open to divers for just five years. It was previously closed to divers because of hostility between them and the local fishermen. To establish better relations between us I always offer to lift any lobster pots that are stuck fast on the sea bed, and I generally get an enthusiastic response. Parking for both cars and trailers is right next to the slip and is £1.50 for each. There are also toilets in the car park and a few shops and cafés within two minutes walk. A note for dog owners: Sennen beach is out of bounds for dogs between Easter and October.

Hayle

01736 754043

The harbour slip can be found by crossing the old iron swing-bridge at the end of the high street. It is immediately on the left over the bridge. Usable three hours each side of high water with plenty of parking, it can get quite busy in the summer months. The estuary can get very shallow at low water. There is also a vicious sand bar at the entrance to the channel. If there is any sea running large breakers can be found on the bar. It is worth visiting the harbour-master when using the slip for the first time - he has a permanent camera overlooking the sand bar.

Newquay Harbour

01637 872809

The only place from which to launch RIBs is a sandy beach near Newquay Harbour. It is found north-east of town and access is via a steep, narrow road which can get very congested in the summer. It requires a four-wheel drive vehicle and costs £2.70. There are toilets and parking nearby - £2 a car and £3.20 for a trailer. A safety briefing from the harbour-master is required who will also check that you have adequate safety equipment on board (flares, VHF radio, engine spares etc). There is a 4 knot speed limit in the harbour.

Rock

01208 862431

The slip can be found by going through Rock village and following signs to the ferry. Harbour dues are payable to the beach-master at the top of the slip and depend upon boat length and engine

size. They are available at daily, weekly or annual rates. There is a total of three slipways which all end in soft mud. They are usable three hours either side of high water. Public toilets are in Quarry Car Park near Ferry Point. Car parking is free on the road but this will be full by 9.30am in July and August. There is a pay and display car park at Ferry Point. Trailers can be parked on the beach although they will be completely immersed on a spring high tide. The tide can be very strong on the flood and ebb (5-8 knots). This can create a standing wave at Doom Bar which has claimed a number lives over the years. Local advice

is, on returning from open sea, to tuck just inside of the port buoy to avoid the overfall which is virtually invisible from the seaward side.

Padstow

There is a very sheltered slipway found just opposite the harbour-master's office. Launching is £5 per day and trailer parking £3 per day. Padstow has plenty of pubs, cafés and shops close by. There is a 5 knot speed limit through the moorings and the slip can be used two hours either side of high water. In the summer months Padstow gets very busy.

Divers surface

Boat Charter (also see Dive shops)

Day Boats

From Looe
Looe Diver 1 & 2, Sea Urchin and
Morning Glory
Tel: 01503 262727

From Falmouth
Patrice 11   Tel: 01326 313265
Haven Diver   Tel: 01326 210296
Spirit of Cornwall Tel: 01326 231589
Under Pressure   Tel: 01326 311265
Cornish Diver RIB (also north coast)
Tel: 01326 311265

From Helford
Shiralee   Tel: 01326 221446
Blue Minstrel   Tel: 01326 250352

From Porthkerris
Celtic Cat, Balastic RIB and
Predator RIB
Tel: 01326 280620

From Porthoustock Cove

Dive Action   Tel: 01326 280719
Dive Action RIBs   Tel: 01326 280719

From Porthleven
Siteseeker   Tel: 01736 763551

From Penzance

Son Calou   Tel: 01326 752135

Pamela P   Tel: 01736 364182

From Hayle
San Pablo lll   Tel: 01209 716970
Mob: 07974 409567

From Newquay
Atlantic Diver   Tel: 01637 850930
Kool Air RIB   Tel: 01637 872591
Mob: 07855 262899

Liveaboards

MV Maureen, Dartmouth
Tel: 01803 835449

Katrina Thomsen, Plymouth to
Penzance   Tel: 01548 821537
McGregor, Looe   Tel: 01503 263584
Mob: 07774 148399

Travel and accommodation

Cornwall Tourist Board
Tel: 01872 322900

Launceston Tourist Information
Centre
Market House Arcade, Market Street,
Launceston, Cornwall PL15 8EP
Tel: 01566 772321

Liskeard Tourist Information Centre
Foresters Hall, Pike Street, Liskeard,
Cornwall PL14 3JE
Tel: 01579 349148

Bodmin Tourist Information Centre
Shire Hall, Mount Folly Square,
Bodmin, Cornwall PL31 2DB
Tel: 01208 76616

Looe Tourist Information Centre
The Guildhall, Fore Street, Looe,
Cornwall PL13 1AA
Tel: 01503 262072

St Austel Tourist Information Centre
By-Pass Service Station,
Southbourne Road, St Austell,
Cornwall PL25 4RS
Tel: 01726 76333

Truro Tourist Information Centre
Municipal Building, Boscawen Street,
Cornwall TR1 2NE
Tel: 01872 274555

Falmouth Tourist Information Centre
28 Killigrew Street, Falmouth,
Cornwall TR11 3PN
Tel: 01326 312300

Helston and Lizard Tourist
Information Centre
79 Meneage Street, Helston,
Cornwall TR13 8RB
Tel: 01326 565431

Penzance Tourist Information Centre
Station Approach, Penzance,
Cornwall TR18 2NF
Tel: 01736 362207

St Agnes Tourist Information Centre
20 Churchtown, St Agnes, Cornwall
TR5 0QW   Tel: 01872 554150

St Ives Tourist Information Centre
The Guildhall, Street-an-Pol,
Cornwall   Tel: 01736 796297

St Just Library and Tourist
Information Centre
Market Street, St Just, Penzance,
Cornwall TR19 7HX
Tel: 01736 788669

Newquay Tourist Information Centre
Municipal Offices, Marcus Hill,
Newquay, Cornwall TR7 1BD
Tel: 01637 854020

Padstow Tourist Information Centre
Red Brick Building, North Quay,
Padstow, Cornwall PL28 8AF
Tel:01841 533449

Wadebridge Tourist Information
Centre
Eddystone Road, Wadebridge,
Cornwall PL27 6AL
Tel: 01208 813725

Camelford Tourist Information
Centre
North Cornwall Museum, The Clease,
Camelford, Cornwall PL32 9PL
Tel: 01840 212954

View from Sennen looking towards the Brisons

Safety first

Coastguard

Brixham Coastguard:
            01803 882704 and VHF Ch16
Falmouth Coastguard:
            01326 317575 and VHF Ch16
Maritime & Coastguard Agency
National Diving Liaison Officer
MRCC Falmouth, Pendennis Point, Castle
Drive, Falmouth, Cornwall TR11 4AR
www.ken_bazeley@mcga.gov.uk

When contemplating going for a dive there are a few things to consider. Below is the advice from Ken Bazeley, National Diving Liaison Officer for HM Coastguard. Ken is a BSAC Advanced Instructor with 33 years diving experience and reviews all incidents co-ordinated by the Coastguard Service.

First Plan

For local information on weather conditions call the local coastguard. Consider other options and locations if the weather is not considered fair for your trip. With the boat loaded and launched, call your local coastguard station to inform them of your trip, give the name of the vessel and the call sign, if known. Give the number of divers and crew, location of the dive and

expected time of completion. Initial call is on VHF Channel 16 or DSC channel 70 - the coastguard station will give you a working channel to pass your information. Call the coastguard station on your return to port - again initially on VHF channel 16.

Radio Check

Things that help your initial logging in with the coastguard are radio checks. These should be done at the beginning of the season or at the commencement of your diving holiday, when a radio engineer has worked on your set or if you are not sure it is working.
Call: 'Falmouth Coastguard (three times) this is (name) (three times). Radio check over.'
The reply will more than likely be:
'(Name) this is Falmouth Coastguard loud and clear (or whatever your signal strength is) and readability over.'
Your reply will be that your 'signal is loud and clear. (Name) out.'
Your radio check is now complete.

Vessel Safety Identification Scheme

This is a free service offered by the coastguard to encourage all club boat owners to register their vessels with their vessel safety identity scheme (CG 66). This scheme gives the coastguard information on your craft and a picture may even be attached. It is all entered into their database, and is available to all of our current 19 coastguard stations in the UK. This means that when you travel with your boat, you can say to the watch-keeper that you are registered with XYZ coastguard station. This can save you time when booking in with a coastguard station as the watch-keeper will ask for a brief description of your craft if it has not been registered previously.

Application forms for the Vessel Safety Identification can be obtained from:
Maritime & Coastguard Agency
Spring Place
105 Commercial Road
Southampton SO15 1EG
Also on the website www.mcga.gov.uk

So you are now out on your dive. On most occasions things go fine, but occasionally things can go wrong and the skipper thinks 'Do I need to contact the coastguard?' IF IN DOUBT, CALL.

You must inform the coastguard about the following:

- An overdue diver
- A diver feeling seriously unwell
- An accident
- A boat engine acting up
- Weather deteriorating
- A collision
- A puncture

The coastguard cannot stress this enough. They are never too busy to talk to you and they will never consider it a waste of their time.
They can put the RNLI, rescue helicopter and coastguard teams on standby if needed. This will save valuable time and could possibly save lives.

Ken Bazeley coordinating a mayday call

Sennen lifeboat

Useful information

Falmouth Coastguard
Tel: 01326 317575

H.M. Coastguard Maritime Rescue
Coordination Centre
Pendennis Point, Falmouth
Tel: 01326 317575
Emergency:
Dial 999 and ask for the coastguard

Coastal weather forecast
BBC Radio 4 VHF   92.4-95.6MHz
Broadcast Times   00:48, 05:35
BBC Radio 4   LW198KHz
Broadcast Times
00:48, 05:35, 12:00, 17:54

BBC Radio Cornwall Redruth
VHF103.9MHz, MF630KHz

Bodmin VHF
95.2MHzMF 657KHz
Mon-Fri at:
07:25, 08:25, 12:25, 16:55, 17:25
Sat at: 07:25 and 13:10
Sun at: 07:25 and 13:05 including
small craft warnings

Pirate FM
VHF 102.2MHz and 102.8Mhz
throughout the day

BT Coastal Radio Station
VHF Start Point   Ch26
Pendennis   Ch62
Land's End   Ch27
Ilfracombe   Ch05 at 07:33
   and 19:33 (UT)
Falmouth Coastguard
Ch16/Ch67 every four hours from 01:40
(two if strong winds)

Admiralty Chart numbers
1267 Falmouth to Plymouth
777 Land's End to Falmouth
2345 Detail of Land's End,
   Runnelstone, Mount's bay
   and Lizard
1149 Pendeen to Trevose Head
1156 Trevose Head to Hartland Point

Ordnance Survey maps
201 Plymouth to Launceston,
   Tavistock and Looe
204 Truro and Falmouth,
   Roseland Peninsula
203 Land's End, Lizard and the
   Isles of Scilly
200 Newquay and Bodmin,
   Camelford and St. Austell
190 Bude and Clovelly

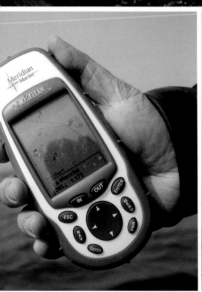

Top: The view from Pendeen lighthouse
Above left: A typical hand-held GPS
Above right: Seven Stones light vessel

Wreck rules

The regulations surrounding wrecks and wreck diving is complex and confusing. A brief summary of the law that may effect diving on wreck sites follows:

Protection of Wrecks Act 1973

Wrecks and wreckage of historical, archaeological or artistic importance may be protected by way of designation under the Protection of Wrecks Act 1973. Under the 1973 Act, it is an offence to carry out certain activities in a defined area surrounding the designated wreck unless a licence for those activities has been obtained from the government. Generally, the relevant government minister must consult appropriate advisors prior to designation, though it is possible to designate a wreck in an emergency without first seeking advice.

The Protection of Wrecks Act is administered by the relevant heritage agency, which seeks advice from the Advisory Committee on Historic Wreck Sites. Licences can be obtained to visit and to carry out survey and excavation work.

Currently, there are 53 sites designated in the UK with a significant number being in Cornish waters. These include:

Coronation (1)(1691) (Penlee Point)
Coronation (2) (1691) (Penlee Point)
Hanover (1763) (Hanover Cove)
Looe Bar Wreck (1684) (Mount's Bay)
Rill Cove Wreck (1616) (Lizard)
Royal Anne (1721) (Lizard)
St Anthony (1527) (Mount's Bay)
Schiedam (1684) (Gunwalloe Cove)

Protection of Military Remains Act 1986

The Protection of Military Remains 1986 Act can be applied both in the UK's terrestrial sea (12 mile limit) and in international waters. In international waters offences under the Act can only be committed by somebody aboard a British-controlled vessel or a British national.

The Ministry of Defence has powers to protect vessels that were in military service within the UK's territorial sea, regardless of nationality. The Ministry of Defence can designate named vessels 'protected places' even if the position of the wreck is not known. All aircraft that have crashed in military service are automatically designated 'protected places'. In addition, the Ministry of Defence can designate wrecks 'controlled sites' where the position is known.

After public consultation the Ministry of Defence has decided to designate 21 wreck sites, 16 'controlled sites, within UK jurisdiction and 5 'protected sites' in international waters.

Merchant Shipping Act 1995 (Re-enacts Pt IX of the 1894 Act)

The ownership of underwater finds that turn out to be 'wreck' is decided according to procedures set out in the Merchant Shipping Act 1995. Finders should assume at the outset that all recovered wreck has an owner. (For the purposes of this Act the term 'wreck' includes jetsam, flotsam, lagan and derelict, it also encompasses aircraft and hovercraft).

Ownership of wreck lies with the original owner or their successor, unless they fail to make a claim to the Receiver of Wreck within one year of notification. Ownership of unclaimed wreck lies in the crown or in a person to whom rights have been granted. In Cornwall the Duchy of Cornwall claims a right of wreck throughout Cornwall.

The Receiver of Wreck has a duty to ensure that finders who report their finds as required receive an appropriate salvage payment. In the case of material considered to be of historic or archaeological importance, a suitable museum is asked to buy the material at the current valuation and the finder receives the net proceeds of the sale as salvage payment. If the right to, or the amount of, salvage cannot be agreed, either between owner and finder or between competing salvors, the Receiver of Wreck will hold the wreck until the matter is settled, either through amicable agreement or court judgement.

Treasure Act 1996
Discoveries in England and Wales over 300 years old that consist mainly of gold or silver and coin hoards are generally 'treasure' for the purposes of the Treasure Act, although objects that are 'wreck' do not count as 'treasure'. If you find treasure, you have to report it to the coroner within 14 days, which will then be subject to a 'treasure inquest'.

The National Heritage Act 2002
This Act harmonises the roles of the UK heritage agencies by extending English Heritage's remit into the marine zone below the low water mark. This means that English Heritage is now the relevant heritage agency responsible for shipwrecks in Cornwall.

Additional reading:

Legal Protection of the Underwater Cultural Heritage.
S. Dromgoole 1999

Taking to the Water
English Heritage 2002

Underwater Finds: Guidance notes for Divers
Joint Nautical Archaeology Policy Committee.

Notes on Wreck Law
Maritime and Coastguard Agency

Useful addresses:

Receiver of Wreck,
The Maritime and Coastguard Agency,
Spring Place,
105 Commercial Road,
Southampton SO15 1EG

Maritime Section,
English Heritage,
National Monuments Record Office,
Kemble Drive,
Swindon
Wilts SN2 2GZ

Dive shops, air/nitrox

Polar Bears
Tel: 01566 773 654 / 776 468
Units B1 – B2, Pennygillam Industrial Estate,
Launceston, Cornwall PL15 7ED
www.polarbears.co.uk
Opening times: 9am-5pm, other times by
arrangement
Services:
• Air to 350BAR
• Servicing of drysuits and wetsuits
• Equipment sales • Equipment hire
They also manufacture drysuits and wetsuits.

Looe Divers

Tel: 01503 262727
Island Court, Marine Drive, Looe, Cornwall
PL13 2DQ
www.looedivers.com
Opening times: 9am-5.30pm, later in the
summer by arrangement
Services:
• Air to 300BAR • Nitrox to 100%
• Training: PADI • RIB diving
• Hard boat charter • Technical diving
• Accommodation • Servicing
• Equipment sale • Equipment hire
This is a very well-equipped diving centre
that also teaches DSAT, DAN, RYA, IANTD
courses. Gear can be washed and left on site
for Looe Divers' customers.

Fowey Diving Services Ltd.
Tel: 01726 833920
21 and 27 Station Road, Fowey,
Cornwall PL23 1DF
www.foweyboathire.freeserve.co.uk
Opening times: 9am-5pm, others times by
arrangement
Services:
• Air to 232bar • Hard boat charter
They are located 100m from the slipway and
car park.

Ocean Sports

Tel: 01726 842817
17 Westend, Pentewan,
Cornwall PL26 6BX
www.ocean-sports.co.uk
Opening times: 9am-5pm, later in the
summer by arrangement
Services:
• Air to 232BAR • Nitrox to 40%
• Training: PADI, BSAC • RIB diving
• Hard boat charter • Accommodation
• Servicing • Equipment sale
• Equipment hire
Try your hand diving with an old Siebe
Gorman hard hat and suit.

Seaways Diving
Tel: 01326 375544
Seaway House, Commercial Road, Penryn,
Cornwall TR10 8AQ
Opening times: 8.30am-5pm, later by
arrangement
Services:
• Air to 320BAR • Nitrox to 100%
• Hard boat charter • Accommodation
• Servicing • Equipment sale
• Cylinder hire
Established in 1980, Seaways is an
equipment servicing specialist and also has
in-house cylinder testing facilities.

Cornish Diving
Tel: 01326 311265/313178
Bar Road, Falmouth, Cornwall TR11 4BN
www.cornishdiving.co.uk
Opening times: 9am-5.30pm, later in the
summer or by arrangement
Services:
• Air to 300BAR • Nitrox to 100%
• Training: PADI • RIB diving
• Hard boat charter
• Technical diving - IANTD, TDI
• Accommodation • Servicing
• Equipment sale • Equipment hire
A comprehensive shop offering all levels of
diving.

Haven Scuba School
Tel: 01726 861727
16 Penhale Gardens, Fraddon,
St Columb, Cornwall TR9 6NZ
www.havenscubaschool.com
Opening times: 9am-5pm, other times by
arrangement
Services:
• Air to 300BAR • Training: PADI
• RIB diving - 10.3m
• Hard boat charter • Accommodation
• Servicing • Equipment sale
• Equipment hire
A variety of water sports are available at this
family beach with café and entertainment
facilities. They also travel to Sark, the
Channel Islands and North Cornwall by RIB.

Dive Action Diving Services
Tel: 01326 280719
Unit 2c, Industrial Estate, St.Keverne,
Helston, Cornwall TR12 6PE
www.divecornwall.co.uk
Opening times: 8am-6pm, later over holidays
Services:
• Air to 300BAR • Nitrox to 100%
• Training: PADI, BSAC
• RIB diving - 3 boats • Hard boat charter
• Technical diving - TDI, IANTD
• Accommodation
• Servicing - cylinder testing
• Equipment sales • Equipment hire
Other courses include rebreathers, RYA boat
handling and underwater photography. Trimix
and argon gas are also available. There is a
recompression station on site. They also dive
out of Penzance, Sennen and the north coast.
RIB launch/recover costs £5 per day.

Porthkerris Divers – Land and Sea Sports

Tel: 01326 280620/280877
Porthkerris, St Keverne, Helston,
Cornwall TR12 6QJ
www.porthkerris.com
Opening times: 9am-5pm or when every one
leaves the beach, and in the morning they
open early if pre-arranged
Services:
- Air to 300BAR   • Nitrox to 100%
- Training: PADI
- RIB diving - shuttle service or daily hire,
two RIBs
- Hard boat charter - daily charter, two or
three dives a day
- Technical diving – TDI
- Accommodation and camping is permitted
on their beach
- Servicing – drysuit repairs and general
equipment maintenance.
- Equipment sales   • Equipment hire
Facilities include the Conservatory
Restaurant and launching (£10 per day and
overnight mooring). This is an excellent
family location with beautiful walks and
beach fronts. There is even a children's
adventure playground and a small zoo
including caged monkeys, Vietnamese pot-
bellied pigs and an adjacent ostrich farm.

Sea Acres Diving Centre

Tel: 01326 221446
Sea Acres Holiday Park, Kennack Sands, Ruan
Minor, Helston, Cornwall TR12 7LT
www.lizardiver.co.uk
Opening times: by arrangement, plus drop-
off overnight cylinder service
Services:
- Air to 300BAR   • Nitrox to 100%
- Training: PADI   • Hard boat charter
- Accommodation   • Equipment sales
- Equipment hire
There is a caravan park. They can also
arrange escorted dives on the Royal Anne
Galley, a protected wreck where gold coins
are still found.

Trevair

Tel: 01736 740647
South Treveneague Farm, St Hilary,
Penzance, Cornwall TR20 9BY
Opening times: 9am-6pm or by arrangement
Services:
- Air to 300BAR   • Nitrox to 100%
- Technical diving   • Accommodation
There is camping on site, self-catering
chalets and caravans available. They will give
local GPS positions and marks to divers staying
on site.

Undersea Adventures

Tel: 01736 333040
15a Cuxhaven Way, Long Rock Industrial
Estate, Penzance, Cornwall TR20 8HX
www.undersea.co.uk
Opening times: 9.30am-5.30pm
Monday-Saturday, 9.30am-5.30 (later
by arrangement) 7 days throughout the
summer months
Services:
- Air to 280BAR   • Nitrox to 80%
- Training: PADI   • RIB diving
- Hard boat charter   • Accommodation
- Servicing   • Equipment sales
- Equipment hire

Mount's Bay Diving

Tel: 01736 752135
Albert Pier, Penzance, Cornwall TR27 4BU
Opening times: times are flexible and should
be arranged by telephone
Services:
- Air to 232BAR   • Hard boat charter

Dive St Ives

Tel: 01736 799229
25 The Wharf, St Ives
www.divestives.com
Opening times: 9am-5pm (10.30pm in
the summer)
Services:
- Air to 350BAR   • Nitrox to 50%
- Training: PADI   • RIB diving
- Hard boat charter – 'Our Liz'
- Accommodation   • Servicing
- Equipment sale   • Equipment hire
They will go to the south coast if conditions
are too rough.

Dive Newquay

Tel: 01637 853953
Alexandra Road, Porth, Newquay,
Cornwall PR7 3NA
Opening times: 9am-6pm, also evenings
by arrangement
Services:
- Air to 300BAR   • Nitrox to 100%
- Training: BSAC   • RIB diving
- Technical diving   • Accommodation
- Equipment sales   • Equipment hire
Other: training facilities and pool on site,
will go south coast if too rough.

Kool Air Diving

Tel: 01637 872591
Trelinda Hotel, 20-22 St Georges Road,
Newquay, Cornwall TR7 1RD
www.koolairdiving.com
Opening times: by arrangement
Services:
- Air to 300BAR   • RIB diving
- Accommodation

BSAC Clubs

British Sub-Aqua Club HQ, Telford's Quay, South Pier Road, Ellesmere Port, South Wirral, Cheshire CH65 4FL, Tel: 0151 350 6200. Contact HQ for details on the local clubs below:

Looe, East Cornwall Divers
Austell Mid Cornwall Divers
Truro Duchy Divers
Falmouth Underwater
Falmouth Cornwall Divers SAC
Penzance
Penzance, West Cornwall Divers
Redruth, Peninsula Sub Aqua
Redruth, Tolgus BSAC
Newquay and District
Newquay RAF St Mawgan
Padstow SAC
Bude, Budehaven SAC

ACKNOWLEDGEMENTS
Steve Waring – Wreck researcher and EXUL SAC
Bryan Radford – Buddy – EXUL and Exeter SAC
Mark Webster - Photec
Jamie Howe and Rob Newton – Koolair Diving
Steve Dee – Newquay BSAC
Jon Bass – Looe Divers
John Kendrick – Retired dive boat skipper
Miles Avery - Ocean Sports Pentewan
Andrew McKnight – Mid Cornwall Divers SAC
Ken Bazeley – National Diving Liaison Officer - Maritime & Coastguard Agency